# THE CAMPING Journal

CAMPING, RV AND CARAVAN TRAVEL LOGBOOK

## SECTIONS

**SECTION 1** - CAMPSITE DETAILS AND INFORMATION

**SECTION 2** - CONTACT DETAILS OF FELLOW CAMPERS

**SECTION 3** - PHOTO'S AND OTHER MEMORIES

**SECTION 4** - VEHICLE MAINTENANCE LOGBOOK

Camping Memories

The Life Graduate Publishing Group

No part of this book may be scanned, reproduced or distributed in any printed or electronic form without the prior permission of the author or publisher.

**Copyright - The Life Graduate Publishing Group 2021** - All Rights Reserved

# THE CAMPING Journal

**CAMPING, RV AND CARAVAN TRAVEL LOG**

Hello and welcome!

There's something very special about camping and the opportunity to explore areas of the country or wilderness that you simply can't experience when staying in a resort, hotel or motel.

The freedom to hit the open road with your RV, camper trailer, caravan or your stand-alone tent is exhilarating and the people you meet, the places you visit and the memories created are just so unique.

The Camping Journal has been created using my own camping experiences with family and friends, and I wanted to create a journal for fellow campers to capture the details and adventures from your own camping trips that will become a wonderful reflective journal in the years to come.

Wishing you a wonderful and safe camping experience wherever your journey my take you!

Romney Nelson
Author and Creator of The Camping Journal

CAMPING, RV AND CARAVAN TRAVEL LOG

# THIS CAMPING JOURNAL BELONGS TO:

x x x x x x x x x x x x x x x x x x x x x x x

x x x x x x x x x x x x x x x x x x x x x x x

## STARTING YEAR:

# 20.........

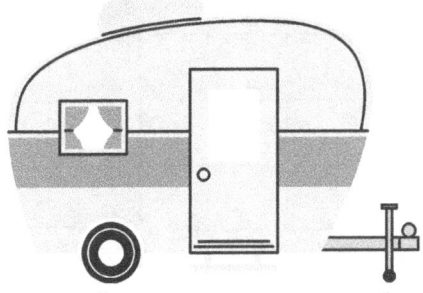

# THE CAMPING
## Journal

TRAVEL DATE/S: _____
DEPARTURE LOCATION: _____
ARRIVAL LOCATION: _____
TOTAL MILAGE: _____ MILES/KM'S:

**WEATHER CONDITIONS ON ARRIVAL:**

TEMP: _____

## CAMPGROUND DETAILS

NAME _____

ADDRESS _____
_____

SITE [ ]   COST [ ]   DAY   WEEK   MONTH

FIRST VISIT   RETURN VISIT

CAMPING GROUND MANAGER [ ]

ALTERNATIVE. SITE FOR NEXT VISIT [ ]

AMENITY BLOCK PASSWORD/CODE [ ]

WIFI PASSWORD/CODE [ ]   FREE   FEE

CAMPING COMPANIONS OR NEW FRIENDS MET

[ ]

CAMPSITE RATING ☆☆☆☆☆
COMMENTS
_____
_____
_____
_____

### EXTRA DETAILS
**POWER**
UN-POWERED
POWERED     15 AMP   30 AMP   50 AMP

**SITE**
LEVEL   UN-LEVEL   REVERSE IN   PULL THROUGH
SUNNY   SHADED   QUIET   NOISY   VIEW

**AMENITIES**
TOILET   SHOWER   WATER   SEWER
CONDITION OF AMENITIES   EXCELLENT   GOOD   POOR

**OTHER**
CHILD FRIENDLY   PET FRIENDLY   PICNIC TABLE
GAMES ROOM   SECURITY   WIFI   T.V
COOKING FACILITIES   CAMP FIRE PERMITTED
HIKING   BEACH   FISHING   RIVER   LAKE
POOL   PLAYGROUND   SPORTS GROUND   GOLF

OTHER: _____

CONVENIENCE STORE     FUEL AVAILABLE
LAUNDRY FACILITIES    CAFE/RESTAURANT

### OTHER INFORMATION OR DETAILS
_____
_____
_____
_____

# CAMPING DETAILS AND EXPERIENCES

**PLACES VISITED AND/OR ACTIVITIES COMPLETED**

_____
_____
_____
_____
_____
_____
_____
_____
_____

**MEMORABLE MOMENTS AND THE HIGHLIGHTS TO REMEMBER**

_____
_____
_____
_____
_____
_____
_____
_____

**WE MUST REMEMBER TO DO THIS NEXT TIME...!**

_____
_____

**INCLUDE A PHOTO, CONTACT DETAILS OF OTHER CAMPERS OR OTHER INFORMATION HERE:**

# THE CAMPING Journal

TRAVEL DATE/S: _____
DEPARTURE LOCATION: _____
ARRIVAL LOCATION: _____
TOTAL MILAGE: _____ MILES/KM'S:

**WEATHER CONDITIONS ON ARRIVAL:**

☀️ ⛅ 🌧️ 💨 ❄️ 🌦️

TEMP: _____

## CAMPGROUND DETAILS

NAME _____

ADDRESS _____
_____

SITE [ ]   COST [ ]   DAY ○ WEEK ○ MONTH ○
FIRST VISIT ○   RETURN VISIT ○
CAMPING GROUND MANAGER [ ]
ALTERNATIVE. SITE FOR NEXT VISIT [ ]
AMENITY BLOCK PASSWORD/CODE [ ]
WIFI PASSWORD/CODE [ ]   FREE ○ FEE ○

CAMPING COMPANIONS OR NEW FRIENDS MET

[                                              ]

CAMPSITE RATING ☆☆☆☆☆
COMMENTS
_____
_____
_____
_____

### EXTRA DETAILS

**POWER**
UN-POWERED ○
POWERED ○   15 AMP ○   30 AMP ○   50 AMP ○

**SITE**
LEVEL ○   UN-LEVEL ○   REVERSE IN ○   PULL THROUGH ○
SUNNY ○   SHADED ○   QUIET ○   NOISY ○   VIEW ○

**AMENITIES**
TOILET ○   SHOWER ○   WATER ○   SEWER ○
CONDITION OF AMENITIES   EXCELLENT ○   GOOD ○   POOR ○

**OTHER**
CHILD FRIENDLY ○   PET FRIENDLY ○   PICNIC TABLE ○
GAMES ROOM ○   SECURITY ○   WIFI ○   T.V ○
COOKING FACILITIES ○   CAMP FIRE PERMITTED ○
HIKING ○   BEACH ○   FISHING ○   RIVER ○   LAKE ○
POOL ○   PLAYGROUND ○   SPORTS GROUND ○   GOLF ○
OTHER: _____
CONVENIENCE STORE ○   FUEL AVAILABLE ○
LAUNDRY FACILITIES ○   CAFE/RESTAURANT ○

### OTHER INFORMATION OR DETAILS

_____
_____
_____
_____

# CAMPING DETAILS AND EXPERIENCES

## PLACES VISITED AND/OR ACTIVITIES COMPLETED

_____
_____
_____
_____
_____
_____
_____
_____
_____
_____

## MEMORABLE MOMENTS AND THE HIGHLIGHTS TO REMEMBER

_____
_____
_____
_____
_____
_____
_____
_____
_____

## WE MUST REMEMBER TO DO THIS NEXT TIME...!

_____
_____
_____

## INCLUDE A PHOTO, CONTACT DETAILS OF OTHER CAMPERS OR OTHER INFORMATION HERE:

# THE CAMPING Journal

TRAVEL DATE/S: _____
DEPARTURE LOCATION: _____
ARRIVAL LOCATION: _____
TOTAL MILAGE: _____ MILES/KM'S:

**WEATHER CONDITIONS ON ARRIVAL:**

TEMP: _____

## CAMPGROUND DETAILS

NAME _____

ADDRESS _____
_____

SITE [ ]   COST [ ]   DAY   WEEK   MONTH

FIRST VISIT   RETURN VISIT

CAMPING GROUND MANAGER [ ]

ALTERNATIVE. SITE FOR NEXT VISIT [ ]

AMENITY BLOCK PASSWORD/CODE [ ]

WIFI PASSWORD/CODE [ ]   FREE   FEE

CAMPING COMPANIONS OR NEW FRIENDS MET

[ ]

CAMPSITE RATING ☆☆☆☆☆

COMMENTS
_____
_____
_____
_____

### EXTRA DETAILS

**POWER**
UN-POWERED
POWERED   15 AMP   30 AMP   50 AMP

**SITE**
LEVEL   UN-LEVEL   REVERSE IN   PULL THROUGH
SUNNY   SHADED   QUIET   NOISY   VIEW

**AMENITIES**
TOILET   SHOWER   WATER   SEWER
CONDITION OF AMENITIES   EXCELLENT   GOOD   POOR

**OTHER**
CHILD FRIENDLY   PET FRIENDLY   PICNIC TABLE
GAMES ROOM   SECURITY   WIFI   T.V
COOKING FACILITIES   CAMP FIRE PERMITTED
HIKING   BEACH   FISHING   RIVER   LAKE
POOL   PLAYGROUND   SPORTS GROUND   GOLF

OTHER: _____

CONVENIENCE STORE        FUEL AVAILABLE
LAUNDRY FACILITIES        CAFE/RESTAURANT

### OTHER INFORMATION OR DETAILS
_____
_____
_____
_____

# CAMPING DETAILS AND EXPERIENCES

**PLACES VISITED AND/OR ACTIVITIES COMPLETED**

_____
_____
_____
_____
_____
_____
_____
_____
_____
_____

**MEMORABLE MOMENTS AND THE HIGHLIGHTS TO REMEMBER**

_____
_____
_____
_____
_____
_____
_____
_____

**WE MUST REMEMBER TO DO THIS NEXT TIME...!**

_____
_____
_____

**INCLUDE A PHOTO, CONTACT DETAILS OF OTHER CAMPERS OR OTHER INFORMATION HERE:**

# THE CAMPING Journal

TRAVEL DATE/S: _____
DEPARTURE LOCATION: _____
ARRIVAL LOCATION: _____
TOTAL MILAGE: _____ MILES/KM'S:

**WEATHER CONDITIONS ON ARRIVAL:**
☀️ ⛅ 🌧️ 💨 ❄️ 🌦️

TEMP: _____

## CAMPGROUND DETAILS

NAME _____

ADDRESS _____

SITE [ ] COST [ ] DAY ○ WEEK ○ MONTH ○

FIRST VISIT ○  RETURN VISIT ○

CAMPING GROUND MANAGER [ ]

ALTERNATIVE. SITE FOR NEXT VISIT [ ]

AMENITY BLOCK PASSWORD/CODE [ ]

WIFI PASSWORD/CODE [ ]  FREE ○ FEE ○

CAMPING COMPANIONS OR NEW FRIENDS MET

CAMPSITE RATING ☆☆☆☆☆
COMMENTS
_____
_____
_____
_____
_____

### EXTRA DETAILS

**POWER**
UN-POWERED ○
POWERED ○  15 AMP ○  30 AMP ○  50 AMP ○

**SITE**
LEVEL ○  UN-LEVEL ○  REVERSE IN ○  PULL THROUGH ○
SUNNY ○  SHADED ○  QUIET ○  NOISY ○  VIEW ○

**AMENITIES**
TOILET ○  SHOWER ○  WATER ○  SEWER ○
CONDITION OF AMENITIES  EXCELLENT ○  GOOD ○  POOR ○

**OTHER**
CHILD FRIENDLY ○  PET FRIENDLY ○  PICNIC TABLE ○
GAMES ROOM ○  SECURITY ○  WIFI ○  T.V ○
COOKING FACILITIES ○  CAMP FIRE PERMITTED ○
HIKING ○  BEACH ○  FISHING ○  RIVER ○  LAKE ○
POOL ○  PLAYGROUND ○  SPORTS GROUND ○  GOLF ○
OTHER: _____
CONVENIENCE STORE ○   FUEL AVAILABLE ○
LAUNDRY FACILITIES ○   CAFE/RESTAURANT ○

### OTHER INFORMATION OR DETAILS
_____
_____
_____
_____

# CAMPING DETAILS AND EXPERIENCES
✗ ✗ ✗ ✗ ✗ ✗ ✗ ✗ ✗ ✗ ✗ ✗ ✗ ✗ ✗ ✗ ✗ ✗ ✗ ✗ ✗ ✗ ✗ ✗ ✗ ✗

## PLACES VISITED AND/OR ACTIVITIES COMPLETED 🚶

_____
_____
_____
_____
_____
_____
_____
_____
_____
_____

## MEMORABLE MOMENTS AND THE HIGHLIGHTS TO REMEMBER 🙌

_____
_____
_____
_____
_____
_____
_____
_____
_____

## WE MUST REMEMBER TO DO THIS NEXT TIME...! ☑

_____
_____
_____

## INCLUDE A PHOTO, CONTACT DETAILS OF OTHER CAMPERS OR OTHER INFORMATION HERE:

# THE CAMPING Journal

TRAVEL DATE/S: _____
DEPARTURE LOCATION: _____
ARRIVAL LOCATION: _____
TOTAL MILAGE: _____ MILES/KM'S:

## WEATHER CONDITIONS ON ARRIVAL:

☀️ ⛅ 🌧️ 💨 ❄️ 🌦️

TEMP: _____

## CAMPGROUND DETAILS

NAME _____
ADDRESS _____
_____

SITE [ ]     COST [ ]     ○ DAY  ○ WEEK  ○ MONTH
○ FIRST VISIT     ○ RETURN VISIT
CAMPING GROUND MANAGER [ ]
ALTERNATIVE. SITE FOR NEXT VISIT [ ]
AMENITY BLOCK PASSWORD/CODE [ ]
WIFI PASSWORD/CODE [ ]     ○ FREE  ○ FEE

CAMPING COMPANIONS OR NEW FRIENDS MET
[                                                    ]

CAMPSITE RATING ☆☆☆☆☆
COMMENTS
_____
_____
_____
_____

### EXTRA DETAILS

**POWER**
UN-POWERED ○
POWERED ○     ○ 15 AMP   ○ 30 AMP   ○ 50 AMP

**SITE**
LEVEL ○   UN-LEVEL ○   REVERSE IN ○   PULL THROUGH ○
SUNNY ○   SHADED ○   QUIET ○   NOISY ○   VIEW ○

**AMENITIES**
TOILET ○   SHOWER ○   WATER ○   SEWER ○
CONDITION OF AMENITIES   EXCELLENT ○   GOOD ○   POOR ○

**OTHER**
CHILD FRIENDLY ○   PET FRIENDLY ○   PICNIC TABLE ○
GAMES ROOM ○   SECURITY ○   WIFI ○   T.V ○
COOKING FACILITIES ○   CAMP FIRE PERMITTED ○
HIKING ○   BEACH ○   FISHING ○   RIVER ○   LAKE ○
POOL ○   PLAYGROUND ○   SPORTS GROUND ○   GOLF ○

OTHER: _____

CONVENIENCE STORE ○       FUEL AVAILABLE ○
LAUNDRY FACILITIES ○      CAFE/RESTAURANT ○

### OTHER INFORMATION OR DETAILS
_____
_____
_____
_____

# CAMPING DETAILS AND EXPERIENCES

## PLACES VISITED AND/OR ACTIVITIES COMPLETED

## MEMORABLE MOMENTS AND THE HIGHLIGHTS TO REMEMBER

## WE MUST REMEMBER TO DO THIS NEXT TIME...!

INCLUDE A PHOTO, CONTACT DETAILS OF OTHER CAMPERS OR OTHER INFORMATION HERE:

# THE CAMPING Journal

TRAVEL DATE/S: _____
DEPARTURE LOCATION: _____
ARRIVAL LOCATION: _____
TOTAL MILAGE: _____ MILES/KM'S:

## WEATHER CONDITIONS ON ARRIVAL:

TEMP: _____

## CAMPGROUND DETAILS

NAME _____

ADDRESS _____
_____

SITE [ ]   COST [ ]   DAY   WEEK   MONTH

FIRST VISIT   RETURN VISIT

CAMPING GROUND MANAGER [ ]

ALTERNATIVE. SITE FOR NEXT VISIT [ ]

AMENITY BLOCK PASSWORD/CODE [ ]

WIFI PASSWORD/CODE [ ]   FREE   FEE

CAMPING COMPANIONS OR NEW FRIENDS MET

[ ]

CAMPSITE RATING ☆☆☆☆☆

COMMENTS
_____
_____
_____
_____

## EXTRA DETAILS

### POWER
UN-POWERED
POWERED   15 AMP   30 AMP   50 AMP

### SITE
LEVEL   UN-LEVEL   REVERSE IN   PULL THROUGH
SUNNY   SHADED   QUIET   NOISY   VIEW

### AMENITIES
TOILET   SHOWER   WATER   SEWER
CONDITION OF AMENITIES   EXCELLENT   GOOD   POOR

### OTHER
CHILD FRIENDLY   PET FRIENDLY   PICNIC TABLE
GAMES ROOM   SECURITY   WIFI   T.V
COOKING FACILITIES   CAMP FIRE PERMITTED
HIKING   BEACH   FISHING   RIVER   LAKE
POOL   PLAYGROUND   SPORTS GROUND   GOLF
OTHER: _____
CONVENIENCE STORE   FUEL AVAILABLE
LAUNDRY FACILITIES   CAFE/RESTAURANT

## OTHER INFORMATION OR DETAILS
_____
_____
_____
_____

# CAMPING DETAILS AND EXPERIENCES

## PLACES VISITED AND/OR ACTIVITIES COMPLETED
_____
_____
_____
_____
_____
_____
_____
_____
_____

## MEMORABLE MOMENTS AND THE HIGHLIGHTS TO REMEMBER
_____
_____
_____
_____
_____
_____
_____
_____

## WE MUST REMEMBER TO DO THIS NEXT TIME…!
_____
_____
_____

### INCLUDE A PHOTO, CONTACT DETAILS OF OTHER CAMPERS OR OTHER INFORMATION HERE:

# THE CAMPING Journal

TRAVEL DATE/S: _____
DEPARTURE LOCATION: _____
ARRIVAL LOCATION: _____
TOTAL MILAGE: _____ MILES/KM'S:

## WEATHER CONDITIONS ON ARRIVAL:

☀️  ⛅  🌧️  🌬️  ❄️  🌦️

TEMP: _____

## CAMPGROUND DETAILS

NAME _____

ADDRESS _____
_____

SITE [ ]   COST [ ]   DAY ○ WEEK ○ MONTH ○

FIRST VISIT ○   RETURN VISIT ○

CAMPING GROUND MANAGER [ _____ ]

ALTERNATIVE. SITE FOR NEXT VISIT [ _____ ]

AMENITY BLOCK PASSWORD/CODE [ _____ ]

WIFI PASSWORD/CODE [ _____ ]   FREE ○   FEE ○

CAMPING COMPANIONS OR NEW FRIENDS MET

[                                                      ]

CAMPSITE RATING ☆☆☆☆☆

COMMENTS
_____
_____
_____
_____

### EXTRA DETAILS

**POWER**
UN-POWERED ○
POWERED ○    15 AMP ○   30 AMP ○   50 AMP ○

**SITE**
LEVEL ○   UN-LEVEL ○   REVERSE IN ○   PULL THROUGH ○
SUNNY ○   SHADED ○   QUIET ○   NOISY ○   VIEW ○

**AMENITIES**
TOILET ○   SHOWER ○   WATER ○   SEWER ○
CONDITION OF AMENITIES   EXCELLENT ○   GOOD ○   POOR ○

**OTHER**
CHILD FRIENDLY ○   PET FRIENDLY ○   PICNIC TABLE ○
GAMES ROOM ○   SECURITY ○   WIFI ○   T.V ○
COOKING FACILITIES ○   CAMP FIRE PERMITTED ○
HIKING ○   BEACH ○   FISHING ○   RIVER ○   LAKE ○
POOL ○   PLAYGROUND ○   SPORTS GROUND ○   GOLF ○

OTHER: _____

CONVENIENCE STORE ○         FUEL AVAILABLE ○
LAUNDRY FACILITIES ○         CAFE/RESTAURANT ○

### OTHER INFORMATION OR DETAILS

_____
_____
_____
_____

# THE CAMPING Journal

# CAMPING DETAILS AND EXPERIENCES
× × × × × × × × × × × × × × × × × × × × × × × ×

## PLACES VISITED AND/OR ACTIVITIES COMPLETED

_____
_____
_____
_____
_____
_____
_____
_____
_____
_____

## MEMORABLE MOMENTS AND THE HIGHLIGHTS TO REMEMBER

_____
_____
_____
_____
_____
_____
_____
_____
_____

## WE MUST REMEMBER TO DO THIS NEXT TIME...!

_____
_____
_____

## INCLUDE A PHOTO, CONTACT DETAILS OF OTHER CAMPERS OR OTHER INFORMATION HERE:

# THE CAMPING Journal

TRAVEL DATE/S: _____
DEPARTURE LOCATION: _____
ARRIVAL LOCATION: _____
TOTAL MILAGE: _____ MILES/KM'S:

## WEATHER CONDITIONS ON ARRIVAL:

☀️ ⛅ 🌧️ 💨 ❄️ 🌦️

TEMP: _____

## CAMPGROUND DETAILS

NAME _____

ADDRESS _____
_____

SITE [ ]   COST [ ]   DAY ○ WEEK ○ MONTH ○

FIRST VISIT ○   RETURN VISIT ○

CAMPING GROUND MANAGER [ ]

ALTERNATIVE. SITE FOR NEXT VISIT [ ]

AMENITY BLOCK PASSWORD/CODE [ ]

WIFI PASSWORD/CODE [ ]   FREE ○ FEE ○

CAMPING COMPANIONS OR NEW FRIENDS MET

[                                    ]

CAMPSITE RATING ☆☆☆☆☆

COMMENTS
_____
_____
_____
_____

### EXTRA DETAILS

**POWER**
UN-POWERED ○
POWERED ○   15 AMP ○   30 AMP ○   50 AMP ○

**SITE**
LEVEL ○   UN-LEVEL ○   REVERSE IN ○   PULL THROUGH ○
SUNNY ○   SHADED ○   QUIET ○   NOISY ○   VIEW ○

**AMENITIES**
TOILET ○   SHOWER ○   WATER ○   SEWER ○
CONDITION OF AMENITIES   EXCELLENT ○   GOOD ○   POOR ○

**OTHER**
CHILD FRIENDLY ○   PET FRIENDLY ○   PICNIC TABLE ○
GAMES ROOM ○   SECURITY ○   WIFI ○   T.V ○
COOKING FACILITIES ○   CAMP FIRE PERMITTED ○
HIKING ○   BEACH ○   FISHING ○   RIVER ○   LAKE ○
POOL ○   PLAYGROUND ○   SPORTS GROUND ○   GOLF ○

OTHER: _____

CONVENIENCE STORE ○   FUEL AVAILABLE ○
LAUNDRY FACILITIES ○   CAFE/RESTAURANT ○

### OTHER INFORMATION OR DETAILS
_____
_____
_____
_____

# CAMPING DETAILS AND EXPERIENCES
x x x x x x x x x x x x x x x x x x x x x

**PLACES VISITED AND/OR ACTIVITIES COMPLETED** 🚶

_____
_____
_____
_____
_____
_____
_____
_____
_____
_____

**MEMORABLE MOMENTS AND THE HIGHLIGHTS TO REMEMBER** 👏

_____
_____
_____
_____
_____
_____
_____
_____

**WE MUST REMEMBER TO DO THIS NEXT TIME...!** ✅

_____
_____
_____

**INCLUDE A PHOTO, CONTACT DETAILS OF OTHER CAMPERS OR OTHER INFORMATION HERE:**

# THE CAMPING Journal

TRAVEL DATE/S: _____
DEPARTURE LOCATION: _____
ARRIVAL LOCATION: _____
TOTAL MILAGE: _____ MILES/KM'S:

**WEATHER CONDITIONS ON ARRIVAL:**

☀️ ⛅ ⛈️ 🌬️ ❄️ 🌦️

TEMP: _____

## CAMPGROUND DETAILS

NAME _____

ADDRESS _____
_____

SITE [ ]   COST [ ]   ○ DAY  ○ WEEK  ○ MONTH

FIRST VISIT ○   RETURN VISIT ○

CAMPING GROUND MANAGER [_____]

ALTERNATIVE. SITE FOR NEXT VISIT [_____]

AMENITY BLOCK PASSWORD/CODE [_____]

WIFI PASSWORD/CODE [_____]  ○ FREE  ○ FEE

CAMPING COMPANIONS OR NEW FRIENDS MET
[_____
_____
_____]

CAMPSITE RATING ☆☆☆☆☆

COMMENTS
_____
_____
_____
_____

### EXTRA DETAILS

**POWER**
UN-POWERED ○
POWERED ○    ○ 15 AMP   ○ 30 AMP   ○ 50 AMP

**SITE**
○ LEVEL   ○ UN-LEVEL   ○ REVERSE IN   ○ PULL THROUGH
○ SUNNY   ○ SHADED   ○ QUIET   ○ NOISY   ○ VIEW

**AMENITIES**
○ TOILET   ○ SHOWER   ○ WATER   ○ SEWER
CONDITION OF AMENITIES  ○ EXCELLENT  ○ GOOD  ○ POOR

**OTHER**
○ CHILD FRIENDLY   ○ PET FRIENDLY   ○ PICNIC TABLE
○ GAMES ROOM   ○ SECURITY   ○ WIFI   ○ T.V
○ COOKING FACILITIES   ○ CAMP FIRE PERMITTED
○ HIKING   ○ BEACH   ○ FISHING   ○ RIVER   ○ LAKE
○ POOL   ○ PLAYGROUND   ○ SPORTS GROUND   ○ GOLF

OTHER: _____

○ CONVENIENCE STORE         ○ FUEL AVAILABLE
○ LAUNDRY FACILITIES        ○ CAFE/RESTAURANT

### OTHER INFORMATION OR DETAILS
_____
_____
_____
_____

# CAMPING DETAILS AND EXPERIENCES

## PLACES VISITED AND/OR ACTIVITIES COMPLETED

_____
_____
_____
_____
_____
_____
_____
_____
_____
_____

## MEMORABLE MOMENTS AND THE HIGHLIGHTS TO REMEMBER

_____
_____
_____
_____
_____
_____
_____
_____

## WE MUST REMEMBER TO DO THIS NEXT TIME...!

_____
_____
_____

## INCLUDE A PHOTO, CONTACT DETAILS OF OTHER CAMPERS OR OTHER INFORMATION HERE:

# THE CAMPING Journal

TRAVEL DATE/S: _____
DEPARTURE LOCATION: _____
ARRIVAL LOCATION: _____
TOTAL MILAGE: _____ MILES/KM'S:

**WEATHER CONDITIONS ON ARRIVAL:**

TEMP: _____

## CAMPGROUND DETAILS

NAME _____
ADDRESS _____
_____

SITE [ ]   COST [ ]   DAY ○ WEEK ○ MONTH ○
FIRST VISIT ○   RETURN VISIT ○
CAMPING GROUND MANAGER [ ]
ALTERNATIVE. SITE FOR NEXT VISIT [ ]
AMENITY BLOCK PASSWORD/CODE [ ]
WIFI PASSWORD/CODE [ ]   FREE ○ FEE ○

CAMPING COMPANIONS OR NEW FRIENDS MET

CAMPSITE RATING ☆☆☆☆☆
COMMENTS
_____
_____
_____
_____
_____

### EXTRA DETAILS

**POWER**
UN-POWERED ○
POWERED ○   15 AMP ○   30 AMP ○   50 AMP ○

**SITE**
LEVEL ○   UN-LEVEL ○   REVERSE IN ○   PULL THROUGH ○
SUNNY ○   SHADED ○   QUIET ○   NOISY ○   VIEW ○

**AMENITIES**
TOILET ○   SHOWER ○   WATER ○   SEWER ○
CONDITION OF AMENITIES   EXCELLENT ○   GOOD ○   POOR ○

**OTHER**
CHILD FRIENDLY ○   PET FRIENDLY ○   PICNIC TABLE ○
GAMES ROOM ○   SECURITY ○   WIFI ○   T.V ○
COOKING FACILITIES ○   CAMP FIRE PERMITTED ○
HIKING ○   BEACH ○   FISHING ○   RIVER ○   LAKE ○
POOL ○   PLAYGROUND ○   SPORTS GROUND ○   GOLF ○

OTHER: _____
CONVENIENCE STORE ○   FUEL AVAILABLE ○
LAUNDRY FACILITIES ○   CAFE/RESTAURANT ○

### OTHER INFORMATION OR DETAILS
_____
_____
_____
_____

# CAMPING DETAILS AND EXPERIENCES

## PLACES VISITED AND/OR ACTIVITIES COMPLETED

_____
_____
_____
_____
_____
_____
_____
_____
_____
_____

## MEMORABLE MOMENTS AND THE HIGHLIGHTS TO REMEMBER

_____
_____
_____
_____
_____
_____
_____
_____

## WE MUST REMEMBER TO DO THIS NEXT TIME...!

_____
_____
_____

## INCLUDE A PHOTO, CONTACT DETAILS OF OTHER CAMPERS OR OTHER INFORMATION HERE:

# THE CAMPING Journal

TRAVEL DATE/S: _____
DEPARTURE LOCATION: _____
ARRIVAL LOCATION: _____
TOTAL MILAGE: _____ MILES/KM'S

**WEATHER CONDITIONS ON ARRIVAL:**

TEMP: _____

## CAMPGROUND DETAILS

NAME _____
ADDRESS _____
_____

SITE [ ]  COST [ ]  DAY ○ WEEK ○ MONTH ○
FIRST VISIT ○  RETURN VISIT ○
CAMPING GROUND MANAGER [ ]
ALTERNATIVE. SITE FOR NEXT VISIT [ ]
AMENITY BLOCK PASSWORD/CODE [ ]
WIFI PASSWORD/CODE [ ]  FREE ○  FEE ○

**CAMPING COMPANIONS OR NEW FRIENDS MET**

CAMPSITE RATING ☆☆☆☆☆
COMMENTS
_____
_____
_____
_____

### EXTRA DETAILS

**POWER**
UN-POWERED ○
POWERED   15 AMP ○   30 AMP ○   50 AMP ○

**SITE**
LEVEL ○  UN-LEVEL ○  REVERSE IN ○  PULL THROUGH ○
SUNNY ○  SHADED ○  QUIET ○  NOISY ○  VIEW ○

**AMENITIES**
TOILET ○  SHOWER ○  WATER ○  SEWER ○
CONDITION OF AMENITIES  EXCELLENT ○  GOOD ○  POOR ○

**OTHER**
CHILD FRIENDLY ○   PET FRIENDLY ○   PICNIC TABLE ○
GAMES ROOM ○   SECURITY ○   WIFI ○   T.V ○
COOKING FACILITIES ○   CAMP FIRE PERMITTED ○
HIKING ○  BEACH ○  FISHING ○  RIVER ○  LAKE ○
POOL ○  PLAYGROUND ○  SPORTS GROUND ○  GOLF ○
OTHER: _____
CONVENIENCE STORE ○   FUEL AVAILABLE ○
LAUNDRY FACILITIES ○   CAFE/RESTAURANT ○

### OTHER INFORMATION OR DETAILS
_____
_____
_____
_____

# CAMPING DETAILS AND EXPERIENCES

## PLACES VISITED AND/OR ACTIVITIES COMPLETED

_____
_____
_____
_____
_____
_____
_____
_____
_____

## MEMORABLE MOMENTS AND THE HIGHLIGHTS TO REMEMBER

_____
_____
_____
_____
_____
_____
_____
_____

## WE MUST REMEMBER TO DO THIS NEXT TIME...!

_____
_____
_____

## INCLUDE A PHOTO, CONTACT DETAILS OF OTHER CAMPERS OR OTHER INFORMATION HERE:

# THE CAMPING Journal

TRAVEL DATE/S: _____
DEPARTURE LOCATION: _____
ARRIVAL LOCATION: _____
TOTAL MILAGE: _____ MILES/KM'S:

**WEATHER CONDITIONS ON ARRIVAL:**

TEMP: _____

## CAMPGROUND DETAILS

NAME _____

ADDRESS _____

SITE [ ]   COST [ ]   DAY ○  WEEK ○  MONTH ○

FIRST VISIT ○   RETURN VISIT ○

CAMPING GROUND MANAGER [ ]

ALTERNATIVE. SITE FOR NEXT VISIT [ ]

AMENITY BLOCK PASSWORD/CODE [ ]

WIFI PASSWORD/CODE [ ]   FREE ○  FEE ○

CAMPING COMPANIONS OR NEW FRIENDS MET

CAMPSITE RATING ☆☆☆☆☆
COMMENTS
_____
_____
_____
_____
_____

### EXTRA DETAILS

**POWER**
UN-POWERED ○
POWERED ○   15 AMP ○   30 AMP ○   50 AMP ○

**SITE**
LEVEL ○   UN-LEVEL ○   REVERSE IN ○   PULL THROUGH ○
SUNNY ○   SHADED ○   QUIET ○   NOISY ○   VIEW ○

**AMENITIES**
TOILET ○   SHOWER ○   WATER ○   SEWER ○
CONDITION OF AMENITIES   EXCELLENT ○   GOOD ○   POOR ○

**OTHER**
CHILD FRIENDLY ○   PET FRIENDLY ○   PICNIC TABLE ○
GAMES ROOM ○   SECURITY ○   WIFI ○   T.V ○
COOKING FACILITIES ○   CAMP FIRE PERMITTED ○
HIKING ○   BEACH ○   FISHING ○   RIVER ○   LAKE ○
POOL ○   PLAYGROUND ○   SPORTS GROUND ○   GOLF ○
OTHER: _____
CONVENIENCE STORE ○   FUEL AVAILABLE ○
LAUNDRY FACILITIES ○   CAFE/RESTAURANT ○

### OTHER INFORMATION OR DETAILS

_____
_____
_____
_____
_____

# THE CAMPING Journal

## CAMPING DETAILS AND EXPERIENCES

**PLACES VISITED AND/OR ACTIVITIES COMPLETED**

_____
_____
_____
_____
_____
_____
_____
_____
_____

**MEMORABLE MOMENTS AND THE HIGHLIGHTS TO REMEMBER**

_____
_____
_____
_____
_____
_____
_____
_____

**WE MUST REMEMBER TO DO THIS NEXT TIME...!**

_____
_____
_____

**INCLUDE A PHOTO, CONTACT DETAILS OF OTHER CAMPERS OR OTHER INFORMATION HERE:**

# THE CAMPING Journal

TRAVEL DATE/S: _____
DEPARTURE LOCATION: _____
ARRIVAL LOCATION: _____
TOTAL MILAGE: _____ MILES/KM'S:

**WEATHER CONDITIONS ON ARRIVAL:**

☀️ ⛅ ⛈️ 💨 ❄️ 🌦️

TEMP: _____

## CAMPGROUND DETAILS

NAME _____
ADDRESS _____
_____

SITE [　]    COST [　]    DAY   WEEK   MONTH

FIRST VISIT ◯    RETURN VISIT ◯

CAMPING GROUND MANAGER [_____]

ALTERNATIVE. SITE FOR NEXT VISIT [_____]

AMENITY BLOCK PASSWORD/CODE [_____]

WIFI PASSWORD/CODE [_____]   FREE   FEE

CAMPING COMPANIONS OR NEW FRIENDS MET

[                                    ]

CAMPSITE RATING ☆☆☆☆☆
COMMENTS
_____
_____
_____
_____
_____

### EXTRA DETAILS

**POWER**
UN-POWERED ◯
POWERED ◯     15 AMP    30 AMP    50 AMP

**SITE**
LEVEL    UN-LEVEL    REVERSE IN    PULL THROUGH
SUNNY    SHADED    QUIET    NOISY    VIEW

**AMENITIES**
TOILET    SHOWER    WATER    SEWER
CONDITION OF AMENITIES    EXCELLENT    GOOD    POOR

**OTHER**
CHILD FRIENDLY    PET FRIENDLY    PICNIC TABLE
GAMES ROOM    SECURITY    WIFI    T.V
COOKING FACILITIES    CAMP FIRE PERMITTED
HIKING    BEACH    FISHING    RIVER    LAKE
POOL    PLAYGROUND    SPORTS GROUND    GOLF

OTHER: _____
CONVENIENCE STORE        FUEL AVAILABLE
LAUNDRY FACILITIES       CAFE/RESTAURANT

### OTHER INFORMATION OR DETAILS
_____
_____
_____
_____
_____

# THE CAMPING Journal

## CAMPING DETAILS AND EXPERIENCES

**PLACES VISITED AND/OR ACTIVITIES COMPLETED**

_____
_____
_____
_____
_____
_____
_____
_____
_____
_____

**MEMORABLE MOMENTS AND THE HIGHLIGHTS TO REMEMBER**

_____
_____
_____
_____
_____
_____
_____
_____
_____
_____

**WE MUST REMEMBER TO DO THIS NEXT TIME...!**

_____
_____
_____
_____

**INCLUDE A PHOTO, CONTACT DETAILS OF OTHER CAMPERS OR OTHER INFORMATION HERE:**

# THE CAMPING Journal

TRAVEL DATE/S: _____
DEPARTURE LOCATION: _____
ARRIVAL LOCATION: _____
TOTAL MILAGE: _____ MILES/KM'S:

**WEATHER CONDITIONS ON ARRIVAL:**

TEMP: _____

## CAMPGROUND DETAILS

NAME _____

ADDRESS _____
_____

SITE [ ]   COST [ ]   DAY ○  WEEK ○  MONTH ○

FIRST VISIT ○   RETURN VISIT ○

CAMPING GROUND MANAGER [ ]

ALTERNATIVE. SITE FOR NEXT VISIT [ ]

AMENITY BLOCK PASSWORD/CODE [ ]

WIFI PASSWORD/CODE [ ]   FREE ○  FEE ○

CAMPING COMPANIONS OR NEW FRIENDS MET

[ ]

CAMPSITE RATING ☆☆☆☆☆
COMMENTS
_____
_____
_____
_____

### EXTRA DETAILS

**POWER**
UN-POWERED ○
POWERED ○   15 AMP ○   30 AMP ○   50 AMP ○

**SITE**
LEVEL ○   UN-LEVEL ○   REVERSE IN ○   PULL THROUGH ○
SUNNY ○   SHADED ○   QUIET ○   NOISY ○   VIEW ○

**AMENITIES**
TOILET ○   SHOWER ○   WATER ○   SEWER ○
CONDITION OF AMENITIES   EXCELLENT ○   GOOD ○   POOR ○

**OTHER**
CHILD FRIENDLY ○   PET FRIENDLY ○   PICNIC TABLE ○
GAMES ROOM ○   SECURITY ○   WIFI ○   T.V ○
COOKING FACILITIES ○   CAMP FIRE PERMITTED ○
HIKING ○   BEACH ○   FISHING ○   RIVER ○   LAKE ○
POOL ○   PLAYGROUND ○   SPORTS GROUND ○   GOLF ○
OTHER: _____
CONVENIENCE STORE ○   FUEL AVAILABLE ○
LAUNDRY FACILITIES ○   CAFE/RESTAURANT ○

### OTHER INFORMATION OR DETAILS
_____
_____
_____
_____

# CAMPING DETAILS AND EXPERIENCES

## PLACES VISITED AND/OR ACTIVITIES COMPLETED

_____
_____
_____
_____
_____
_____
_____
_____
_____

## MEMORABLE MOMENTS AND THE HIGHLIGHTS TO REMEMBER

_____
_____
_____
_____
_____
_____
_____
_____

## WE MUST REMEMBER TO DO THIS NEXT TIME...!

_____
_____
_____

## INCLUDE A PHOTO, CONTACT DETAILS OF OTHER CAMPERS OR OTHER INFORMATION HERE:

# THE CAMPING Journal

TRAVEL DATE/S:_____
DEPARTURE LOCATION:_____
ARRIVAL LOCATION:_____
TOTAL MILAGE:_____ MILES/KM'S:

**WEATHER CONDITIONS ON ARRIVAL:**

☀️ ⛅ ⛈️ 💨 ❄️ 🌧️

TEMP: _____

## CAMPGROUND DETAILS

NAME _____

ADDRESS _____
_____

SITE [ ]    COST [ ]    DAY ○ WEEK ○ MONTH ○

FIRST VISIT ○    RETURN VISIT ○

CAMPING GROUND MANAGER [_____]

ALTERNATIVE. SITE FOR NEXT VISIT [_____]

AMENITY BLOCK PASSWORD/CODE [_____]

WIFI PASSWORD/CODE [_____]    FREE ○ FEE ○

CAMPING COMPANIONS OR NEW FRIENDS MET
[                                    ]

CAMPSITE RATING ☆☆☆☆☆
COMMENTS
_____
_____
_____
_____

**EXTRA DETAILS**

**POWER**
UN-POWERED ○
POWERED ○    15 AMP ○  30 AMP ○  50 AMP ○

**SITE**
LEVEL ○  UN-LEVEL ○  REVERSE IN ○  PULL THROUGH ○
SUNNY ○  SHADED ○  QUIET ○  NOISY ○  VIEW ○

**AMENITIES**
TOILET ○  SHOWER ○  WATER ○  SEWER ○
CONDITION OF AMENITIES  EXCELLENT ○  GOOD ○  POOR ○

**OTHER**
CHILD FRIENDLY ○  PET FRIENDLY ○  PICNIC TABLE ○
GAMES ROOM ○  SECURITY ○  WIFI ○  T.V ○
COOKING FACILITIES ○  CAMP FIRE PERMITTED ○
HIKING ○  BEACH ○  FISHING ○  RIVER ○  LAKE ○
POOL ○  PLAYGROUND ○  SPORTS GROUND ○  GOLF ○

OTHER:_____

CONVENIENCE STORE ○    FUEL AVAILABLE ○
LAUNDRY FACILITIES ○    CAFE/RESTAURANT ○

**OTHER INFORMATION OR DETAILS**
_____
_____
_____
_____

# THE CAMPING Journal

## CAMPING DETAILS AND EXPERIENCES

**PLACES VISITED AND/OR ACTIVITIES COMPLETED**

_____
_____
_____
_____
_____
_____
_____
_____
_____
_____

**MEMORABLE MOMENTS AND THE HIGHLIGHTS TO REMEMBER**

_____
_____
_____
_____
_____
_____
_____

**WE MUST REMEMBER TO DO THIS NEXT TIME...!**

_____
_____
_____

**INCLUDE A PHOTO, CONTACT DETAILS OF OTHER CAMPERS OR OTHER INFORMATION HERE:**

# THE CAMPING Journal

TRAVEL DATE/S: _____
DEPARTURE LOCATION: _____
ARRIVAL LOCATION: _____
TOTAL MILAGE: _____ MILES/KM'S:

**WEATHER CONDITIONS ON ARRIVAL:**

TEMP: _____

## CAMPGROUND DETAILS

NAME _____

ADDRESS _____
_____

SITE [ ]   COST [ ]   DAY ○ WEEK ○ MONTH ○

FIRST VISIT ○   RETURN VISIT ○

CAMPING GROUND MANAGER [ ]

ALTERNATIVE. SITE FOR NEXT VISIT [ ]

AMENITY BLOCK PASSWORD/CODE [ ]

WIFI PASSWORD/CODE [ ]   FREE ○ FEE ○

CAMPING COMPANIONS OR NEW FRIENDS MET
[                                          ]

CAMPSITE RATING ☆☆☆☆☆
COMMENTS
_____
_____
_____
_____
_____

### EXTRA DETAILS

**POWER**
UN-POWERED ○
POWERED ○   15 AMP ○   30 AMP ○   50 AMP ○

**SITE**
LEVEL ○   UN-LEVEL ○   REVERSE IN ○   PULL THROUGH ○
SUNNY ○   SHADED ○   QUIET ○   NOISY ○   VIEW ○

**AMENITIES**
TOILET ○   SHOWER ○   WATER ○   SEWER ○
CONDITION OF AMENITIES   EXCELLENT ○   GOOD ○   POOR ○

**OTHER**
CHILD FRIENDLY ○   PET FRIENDLY ○   PICNIC TABLE ○
GAMES ROOM ○   SECURITY ○   WIFI ○   T.V ○
COOKING FACILITIES ○   CAMP FIRE PERMITTED ○
HIKING ○   BEACH ○   FISHING ○   RIVER ○   LAKE ○
POOL ○   PLAYGROUND ○   SPORTS GROUND ○   GOLF ○

OTHER: _____

CONVENIENCE STORE ○   FUEL AVAILABLE ○
LAUNDRY FACILITIES ○   CAFE/RESTAURANT ○

### OTHER INFORMATION OR DETAILS
_____
_____
_____
_____

# CAMPING DETAILS AND EXPERIENCES

## PLACES VISITED AND/OR ACTIVITIES COMPLETED

_____
_____
_____
_____
_____
_____
_____
_____
_____
_____

## MEMORABLE MOMENTS AND THE HIGHLIGHTS TO REMEMBER

_____
_____
_____
_____
_____
_____
_____
_____
_____

## WE MUST REMEMBER TO DO THIS NEXT TIME…!

_____
_____
_____

## INCLUDE A PHOTO, CONTACT DETAILS OF OTHER CAMPERS OR OTHER INFORMATION HERE:

# THE CAMPING Journal

TRAVEL DATE/S: _____
DEPARTURE LOCATION: _____
ARRIVAL LOCATION: _____
TOTAL MILAGE: _____ MILES/KM'S:

**WEATHER CONDITIONS ON ARRIVAL:**

TEMP: _____

## CAMPGROUND DETAILS

NAME _____
ADDRESS _____
_____

SITE [ ]   COST [ ]   DAY   WEEK   MONTH
FIRST VISIT   RETURN VISIT
CAMPING GROUND MANAGER [ ]
ALTERNATIVE. SITE FOR NEXT VISIT [ ]
AMENITY BLOCK PASSWORD/CODE [ ]
WIFI PASSWORD/CODE [ ]   FREE   FEE

CAMPING COMPANIONS OR NEW FRIENDS MET

CAMPSITE RATING ☆☆☆☆☆
COMMENTS
_____
_____
_____
_____

### EXTRA DETAILS

**POWER**
UN-POWERED
POWERED    15 AMP   30 AMP   50 AMP

**SITE**
LEVEL   UN-LEVEL   REVERSE IN   PULL THROUGH
SUNNY   SHADED   QUIET   NOISY   VIEW

**AMENITIES**
TOILET   SHOWER   WATER   SEWER
CONDITION OF AMENITIES   EXCELLENT   GOOD   POOR

**OTHER**
CHILD FRIENDLY   PET FRIENDLY   PICNIC TABLE
GAMES ROOM   SECURITY   WIFI   T.V
COOKING FACILITIES   CAMP FIRE PERMITTED
HIKING   BEACH   FISHING   RIVER   LAKE
POOL   PLAYGROUND   SPORTS GROUND   GOLF

OTHER: _____
CONVENIENCE STORE        FUEL AVAILABLE
LAUNDRY FACILITIES        CAFE/RESTAURANT

### OTHER INFORMATION OR DETAILS
_____
_____
_____
_____

# THE CAMPING Journal

# CAMPING DETAILS AND EXPERIENCES

**PLACES VISITED AND/OR ACTIVITIES COMPLETED**

_____
_____
_____
_____
_____
_____
_____
_____
_____
_____

**MEMORABLE MOMENTS AND THE HIGHLIGHTS TO REMEMBER**

_____
_____
_____
_____
_____
_____
_____
_____

**WE MUST REMEMBER TO DO THIS NEXT TIME...!**

_____
_____
_____

**INCLUDE A PHOTO, CONTACT DETAILS OF OTHER CAMPERS OR OTHER INFORMATION HERE:**

# THE CAMPING Journal

TRAVEL DATE/S: _____
DEPARTURE LOCATION: _____
ARRIVAL LOCATION: _____
TOTAL MILAGE: _____ MILES/KM'S:

**WEATHER CONDITIONS ON ARRIVAL:**

☀️ ⛅ 🌧️ 💨 ❄️ 🌦️

TEMP: _____

## CAMPGROUND DETAILS

NAME _____

ADDRESS _____
_____

SITE [ ]   COST [ ]   DAY ○   WEEK ○   MONTH ○

FIRST VISIT ○   RETURN VISIT ○

CAMPING GROUND MANAGER [ ]

ALTERNATIVE. SITE FOR NEXT VISIT [ ]

AMENITY BLOCK PASSWORD/CODE [ ]

WIFI PASSWORD/CODE [ ]   FREE ○   FEE ○

CAMPING COMPANIONS OR NEW FRIENDS MET

[                                              ]

CAMPSITE RATING ☆☆☆☆☆

COMMENTS
_____
_____
_____
_____
_____

### EXTRA DETAILS

**POWER**
UN-POWERED ○
POWERED ○    15 AMP ○   30 AMP ○   50 AMP ○

**SITE**
LEVEL ○   UN-LEVEL ○   REVERSE IN ○   PULL THROUGH ○
SUNNY ○   SHADED ○   QUIET ○   NOISY ○   VIEW ○

**AMENITIES**
TOILET ○   SHOWER ○   WATER ○   SEWER ○
CONDITION OF AMENITIES   EXCELLENT ○   GOOD ○   POOR ○

**OTHER**
CHILD FRIENDLY ○   PET FRIENDLY ○   PICNIC TABLE ○
GAMES ROOM ○   SECURITY ○   WIFI ○   T.V ○
COOKING FACILITIES ○   CAMP FIRE PERMITTED ○
HIKING ○   BEACH ○   FISHING ○   RIVER ○   LAKE ○
POOL ○   PLAYGROUND ○   SPORTS GROUND ○   GOLF ○
OTHER: _____
CONVENIENCE STORE ○        FUEL AVAILABLE ○
LAUNDRY FACILITIES ○        CAFE/RESTAURANT ○

### OTHER INFORMATION OR DETAILS

_____
_____
_____
_____
_____

# CAMPING DETAILS AND EXPERIENCES

## PLACES VISITED AND/OR ACTIVITIES COMPLETED

_____
_____
_____
_____
_____
_____
_____
_____
_____

## MEMORABLE MOMENTS AND THE HIGHLIGHTS TO REMEMBER

_____
_____
_____
_____
_____
_____
_____
_____

## WE MUST REMEMBER TO DO THIS NEXT TIME...!

_____
_____

**INCLUDE A PHOTO, CONTACT DETAILS OF OTHER CAMPERS OR OTHER INFORMATION HERE:**

# THE CAMPING Journal

TRAVEL DATE/S: _____
DEPARTURE LOCATION: _____
ARRIVAL LOCATION: _____
TOTAL MILAGE: _____ MILES/KM'S:

**WEATHER CONDITIONS ON ARRIVAL:**

TEMP: _____

## CAMPGROUND DETAILS

NAME _____

ADDRESS _____
_____

SITE [ ]    COST [ ]    DAY   WEEK   MONTH

FIRST VISIT   RETURN VISIT

CAMPING GROUND MANAGER [ ]

ALTERNATIVE. SITE FOR NEXT VISIT [ ]

AMENITY BLOCK PASSWORD/CODE [ ]

WIFI PASSWORD/CODE [ ]   FREE   FEE

CAMPING COMPANIONS OR NEW FRIENDS MET

CAMPSITE RATING ☆☆☆☆☆

COMMENTS
_____
_____
_____
_____

### EXTRA DETAILS

**POWER**
UN-POWERED
POWERED    15 AMP   30 AMP   50 AMP

**SITE**
LEVEL   UN-LEVEL   REVERSE IN   PULL THROUGH
SUNNY   SHADED   QUIET   NOISY   VIEW

**AMENITIES**
TOILET   SHOWER   WATER   SEWER
CONDITION OF AMENITIES   EXCELLENT   GOOD   POOR

**OTHER**
CHILD FRIENDLY   PET FRIENDLY   PICNIC TABLE
GAMES ROOM   SECURITY   WIFI   T.V
COOKING FACILITIES   CAMP FIRE PERMITTED
HIKING   BEACH   FISHING   RIVER   LAKE
POOL   PLAYGROUND   SPORTS GROUND   GOLF

OTHER: _____

CONVENIENCE STORE        FUEL AVAILABLE
LAUNDRY FACILITIES       CAFE/RESTAURANT

### OTHER INFORMATION OR DETAILS
_____
_____
_____
_____

# THE CAMPING Journal

## CAMPING DETAILS AND EXPERIENCES

**PLACES VISITED AND/OR ACTIVITIES COMPLETED**

_____
_____
_____
_____
_____
_____
_____
_____
_____

**MEMORABLE MOMENTS AND THE HIGHLIGHTS TO REMEMBER**

_____
_____
_____
_____
_____
_____
_____

**WE MUST REMEMBER TO DO THIS NEXT TIME...!**

_____
_____
_____

**INCLUDE A PHOTO, CONTACT DETAILS OF OTHER CAMPERS OR OTHER INFORMATION HERE:**

# THE CAMPING Journal

TRAVEL DATE/S: _____
DEPARTURE LOCATION: _____
ARRIVAL LOCATION: _____
TOTAL MILAGE: _____ MILES/KM'S:

## WEATHER CONDITIONS ON ARRIVAL:

TEMP: _____

## CAMPGROUND DETAILS

NAME _____

ADDRESS _____
_____

SITE [ ]   COST [ ]   DAY   WEEK   MONTH

FIRST VISIT   RETURN VISIT

CAMPING GROUND MANAGER [ ]

ALTERNATIVE. SITE FOR NEXT VISIT [ ]

AMENITY BLOCK PASSWORD/CODE [ ]

WIFI PASSWORD/CODE [ ]   FREE   FEE

CAMPING COMPANIONS OR NEW FRIENDS MET

CAMPSITE RATING ☆☆☆☆☆

COMMENTS
_____
_____
_____
_____
_____

### EXTRA DETAILS

**POWER**
UN-POWERED
POWERED   15 AMP   30 AMP   50 AMP

**SITE**
LEVEL   UN-LEVEL   REVERSE IN   PULL THROUGH
SUNNY   SHADED   QUIET   NOISY   VIEW

**AMENITIES**
TOILET   SHOWER   WATER   SEWER
CONDITION OF AMENITIES   EXCELLENT   GOOD   POOR

**OTHER**
CHILD FRIENDLY   PET FRIENDLY   PICNIC TABLE
GAMES ROOM   SECURITY   WIFI   T.V
COOKING FACILITIES   CAMP FIRE PERMITTED
HIKING   BEACH   FISHING   RIVER   LAKE
POOL   PLAYGROUND   SPORTS GROUND   GOLF
OTHER: _____
CONVENIENCE STORE   FUEL AVAILABLE
LAUNDRY FACILITIES   CAFE/RESTAURANT

### OTHER INFORMATION OR DETAILS
_____
_____
_____
_____
_____

# CAMPING DETAILS AND EXPERIENCES

## PLACES VISITED AND/OR ACTIVITIES COMPLETED

_____
_____
_____
_____
_____
_____
_____
_____
_____
_____
_____

## MEMORABLE MOMENTS AND THE HIGHLIGHTS TO REMEMBER

_____
_____
_____
_____
_____
_____
_____
_____

## WE MUST REMEMBER TO DO THIS NEXT TIME...!

_____
_____
_____

**INCLUDE A PHOTO, CONTACT DETAILS OF OTHER CAMPERS OR OTHER INFORMATION HERE:**

# THE CAMPING Journal

TRAVEL DATE/S: _____
DEPARTURE LOCATION: _____
ARRIVAL LOCATION: _____
TOTAL MILAGE: _____ MILES/KM'S:

## WEATHER CONDITIONS ON ARRIVAL:

☀️ ⛅ 🌧️ 🌬️ ❄️ 🌦️

TEMP: _____

## CAMPGROUND DETAILS

NAME _____

ADDRESS _____
_____

SITE [ ]   COST [ ]   DAY ○ WEEK ○ MONTH ○

FIRST VISIT ○   RETURN VISIT ○

CAMPING GROUND MANAGER [ _____ ]

ALTERNATIVE. SITE FOR NEXT VISIT [ ____ ]

AMENITY BLOCK PASSWORD/CODE [ _____ ]

WIFI PASSWORD/CODE [ _____ ]   FREE ○  FEE ○

CAMPING COMPANIONS OR NEW FRIENDS MET

[ _____ ]

CAMPSITE RATING ☆☆☆☆☆

COMMENTS
_____
_____
_____
_____

### EXTRA DETAILS

**POWER**
UN-POWERED ○
POWERED ○    15 AMP ○   30 AMP ○   50 AMP ○

**SITE**
LEVEL ○   UN-LEVEL ○   REVERSE IN ○   PULL THROUGH ○
SUNNY ○   SHADED ○   QUIET ○   NOISY ○   VIEW ○

**AMENITIES**
TOILET ○   SHOWER ○   WATER ○   SEWER ○
CONDITION OF AMENITIES   EXCELLENT ○   GOOD ○   POOR ○

**OTHER**
CHILD FRIENDLY ○   PET FRIENDLY ○   PICNIC TABLE ○
GAMES ROOM ○   SECURITY ○   WIFI ○   T.V ○
COOKING FACILITIES ○   CAMP FIRE PERMITTED ○
HIKING ○   BEACH ○   FISHING ○   RIVER ○   LAKE ○
POOL ○   PLAYGROUND ○   SPORTS GROUND ○   GOLF ○

OTHER: _____

CONVENIENCE STORE ○        FUEL AVAILABLE ○
LAUNDRY FACILITIES ○       CAFE/RESTAURANT ○

### OTHER INFORMATION OR DETAILS
_____
_____
_____
_____

# THE CAMPING Journal

# CAMPING DETAILS AND EXPERIENCES

**PLACES VISITED AND/OR ACTIVITIES COMPLETED**

_____
_____
_____
_____
_____
_____
_____
_____
_____

**MEMORABLE MOMENTS AND THE HIGHLIGHTS TO REMEMBER**

_____
_____
_____
_____
_____
_____
_____
_____
_____

**WE MUST REMEMBER TO DO THIS NEXT TIME...!**

_____
_____
_____

**INCLUDE A PHOTO, CONTACT DETAILS OF OTHER CAMPERS OR OTHER INFORMATION HERE:**

# THE CAMPING Journal

TRAVEL DATE/S: _____
DEPARTURE LOCATION: _____
ARRIVAL LOCATION: _____
TOTAL MILAGE: _____ MILES/KM'S:

**WEATHER CONDITIONS ON ARRIVAL:**

TEMP: _____

## CAMPGROUND DETAILS

NAME _____

ADDRESS _____
_____

SITE [ ]   COST [ ]   DAY ○ WEEK ○ MONTH ○

FIRST VISIT ○   RETURN VISIT ○

CAMPING GROUND MANAGER [ ]

ALTERNATIVE. SITE FOR NEXT VISIT [ ]

AMENITY BLOCK PASSWORD/CODE [ ]

WIFI PASSWORD/CODE [ ]   FREE ○ FEE ○

CAMPING COMPANIONS OR NEW FRIENDS MET

[ ]

CAMPSITE RATING ☆☆☆☆☆

COMMENTS
_____
_____
_____
_____

### EXTRA DETAILS

**POWER**
UN-POWERED ○
POWERED ○   15 AMP ○   30 AMP ○   50 AMP ○

**SITE**
LEVEL ○   UN-LEVEL ○   REVERSE IN ○   PULL THROUGH ○
SUNNY ○   SHADED ○   QUIET ○   NOISY ○   VIEW ○

**AMENITIES**
TOILET ○   SHOWER ○   WATER ○   SEWER ○
CONDITION OF AMENITIES   EXCELLENT ○   GOOD ○   POOR ○

**OTHER**
CHILD FRIENDLY ○   PET FRIENDLY ○   PICNIC TABLE ○
GAMES ROOM ○   SECURITY ○   WIFI ○   T.V ○
COOKING FACILITIES ○   CAMP FIRE PERMITTED ○
HIKING ○   BEACH ○   FISHING ○   RIVER ○   LAKE ○
POOL ○   PLAYGROUND ○   SPORTS GROUND ○   GOLF ○

OTHER: _____
CONVENIENCE STORE ○   FUEL AVAILABLE ○
LAUNDRY FACILITIES ○   CAFE/RESTAURANT ○

### OTHER INFORMATION OR DETAILS
_____
_____
_____
_____

# CAMPING DETAILS AND EXPERIENCES

## PLACES VISITED AND/OR ACTIVITIES COMPLETED

_____
_____
_____
_____
_____
_____
_____
_____
_____

## MEMORABLE MOMENTS AND THE HIGHLIGHTS TO REMEMBER

_____
_____
_____
_____
_____
_____
_____
_____

## WE MUST REMEMBER TO DO THIS NEXT TIME...!

_____
_____
_____

## INCLUDE A PHOTO, CONTACT DETAILS OF OTHER CAMPERS OR OTHER INFORMATION HERE:

# THE CAMPING
## Journal

TRAVEL DATE/S:_____
DEPARTURE LOCATION:_____
ARRIVAL LOCATION: _____
TOTAL MILAGE: _____ MILES/KM'S:

**WEATHER CONDITIONS ON ARRIVAL:**

TEMP: _____

## CAMPGROUND DETAILS

NAME_____

ADDRESS_____
_____

SITE [  ]   COST [  ]   DAY   WEEK   MONTH

FIRST VISIT   RETURN VISIT

CAMPING GROUND MANAGER [          ]

ALTERNATIVE. SITE FOR NEXT VISIT [    ]

AMENITY BLOCK PASSWORD/CODE [        ]

WIFI PASSWORD/CODE [    ]   FREE   FEE

**CAMPING COMPANIONS OR NEW FRIENDS MET**

[                                           ]

CAMPSITE RATING ☆☆☆☆☆

COMMENTS
_____
_____
_____
_____
_____

### EXTRA DETAILS

**POWER**
UN-POWERED
POWERED    15 AMP   30 AMP   50 AMP

**SITE**
LEVEL   UN-LEVEL   REVERSE IN   PULL THROUGH
SUNNY   SHADED   QUIET   NOISY   VIEW

**AMENITIES**
TOILET   SHOWER   WATER   SEWER
CONDITION OF AMENITIES   EXCELLENT   GOOD   POOR

**OTHER**
CHILD FRIENDLY   PET FRIENDLY   PICNIC TABLE
GAMES ROOM   SECURITY   WIFI   T.V
COOKING FACILITIES   CAMP FIRE PERMITTED
HIKING   BEACH   FISHING   RIVER   LAKE
POOL   PLAYGROUND   SPORTS GROUND   GOLF
OTHER:_____
CONVENIENCE STORE   FUEL AVAILABLE
LAUNDRY FACILITIES   CAFE/RESTAURANT

### OTHER INFORMATION OR DETAILS
_____
_____
_____
_____
_____

# CAMPING DETAILS AND EXPERIENCES

## PLACES VISITED AND/OR ACTIVITIES COMPLETED

_____
_____
_____
_____
_____
_____
_____
_____
_____

## MEMORABLE MOMENTS AND THE HIGHLIGHTS TO REMEMBER

_____
_____
_____
_____
_____
_____
_____

## WE MUST REMEMBER TO DO THIS NEXT TIME...!

_____
_____
_____

## INCLUDE A PHOTO, CONTACT DETAILS OF OTHER CAMPERS OR OTHER INFORMATION HERE:

# THE CAMPING Journal

TRAVEL DATE/S: _____
DEPARTURE LOCATION: _____
ARRIVAL LOCATION: _____
TOTAL MILAGE: _____ MILES/KM'S:

**WEATHER CONDITIONS ON ARRIVAL:**

☀️ ⛅ 🌧️ 💨 ❄️ 🌦️

TEMP: _____

## CAMPGROUND DETAILS

NAME _____

ADDRESS _____
_____

SITE [ ]    COST [ ]    DAY ○ WEEK ○ MONTH ○

FIRST VISIT ○    RETURN VISIT ○

CAMPING GROUND MANAGER [ ]

ALTERNATIVE. SITE FOR NEXT VISIT [ ]

AMENITY BLOCK PASSWORD/CODE [ ]

WIFI PASSWORD/CODE [ ]   FREE ○ FEE ○

**CAMPING COMPANIONS OR NEW FRIENDS MET**
[ ]

CAMPSITE RATING ☆☆☆☆☆

COMMENTS
_____
_____
_____
_____
_____

### EXTRA DETAILS

**POWER**
UN-POWERED ○
POWERED ○    15 AMP ○   30 AMP ○   50 AMP ○

**SITE**
LEVEL ○   UN-LEVEL ○   REVERSE IN ○   PULL THROUGH ○
SUNNY ○   SHADED ○   QUIET ○   NOISY ○   VIEW ○

**AMENITIES**
TOILET ○   SHOWER ○   WATER ○   SEWER ○
CONDITION OF AMENITIES   EXCELLENT ○   GOOD ○   POOR ○

**OTHER**
CHILD FRIENDLY ○   PET FRIENDLY ○   PICNIC TABLE ○
GAMES ROOM ○   SECURITY ○   WIFI ○   T.V ○
COOKING FACILITIES ○   CAMP FIRE PERMITTED ○
HIKING ○   BEACH ○   FISHING ○   RIVER ○   LAKE ○
POOL ○   PLAYGROUND ○   SPORTS GROUND ○   GOLF ○
OTHER: _____
CONVENIENCE STORE ○      FUEL AVAILABLE ○
LAUNDRY FACILITIES ○      CAFE/RESTAURANT ○

### OTHER INFORMATION OR DETAILS
_____
_____
_____
_____
_____

# CAMPING DETAILS AND EXPERIENCES

## PLACES VISITED AND/OR ACTIVITIES COMPLETED 🚶

_____
_____
_____
_____
_____
_____
_____
_____
_____
_____

## MEMORABLE MOMENTS AND THE HIGHLIGHTS TO REMEMBER 🙌

_____
_____
_____
_____
_____
_____
_____

## WE MUST REMEMBER TO DO THIS NEXT TIME...! ✅

_____
_____
_____

## INCLUDE A PHOTO, CONTACT DETAILS OF OTHER CAMPERS OR OTHER INFORMATION HERE:

# THE CAMPING Journal

TRAVEL DATE/S: _____
DEPARTURE LOCATION: _____
ARRIVAL LOCATION: _____
TOTAL MILAGE: _____ MILES/KM'S:

## WEATHER CONDITIONS ON ARRIVAL:

TEMP: _____

## CAMPGROUND DETAILS

NAME _____

ADDRESS _____
_____

SITE [ ]    COST [ ]    DAY  WEEK  MONTH

FIRST VISIT ○    RETURN VISIT ○

CAMPING GROUND MANAGER [ ]

ALTERNATIVE. SITE FOR NEXT VISIT [ ]

AMENITY BLOCK PASSWORD/CODE [ ]

WIFI PASSWORD/CODE [ ]    FREE  FEE

CAMPING COMPANIONS OR NEW FRIENDS MET

[ ]

CAMPSITE RATING ☆☆☆☆☆

COMMENTS
_____
_____
_____
_____

### EXTRA DETAILS

**POWER**
UN-POWERED ○
POWERED ○    15 AMP ○   30 AMP ○   50 AMP ○

**SITE**
LEVEL   UN-LEVEL   REVERSE IN   PULL THROUGH
SUNNY   SHADED   QUIET   NOISY   VIEW

**AMENITIES**
TOILET   SHOWER   WATER   SEWER
CONDITION OF AMENITIES   EXCELLENT   GOOD   POOR

**OTHER**
CHILD FRIENDLY   PET FRIENDLY   PICNIC TABLE
GAMES ROOM   SECURITY   WIFI   T.V
COOKING FACILITIES   CAMP FIRE PERMITTED
HIKING   BEACH   FISHING   RIVER   LAKE
POOL   PLAYGROUND   SPORTS GROUND   GOLF

OTHER: _____

CONVENIENCE STORE        FUEL AVAILABLE
LAUNDRY FACILITIES        CAFE/RESTAURANT

### OTHER INFORMATION OR DETAILS
_____
_____
_____
_____

# CAMPING DETAILS AND EXPERIENCES

## PLACES VISITED AND/OR ACTIVITIES COMPLETED

_____
_____
_____
_____
_____
_____
_____
_____
_____
_____

## MEMORABLE MOMENTS AND THE HIGHLIGHTS TO REMEMBER

_____
_____
_____
_____
_____
_____
_____
_____

## WE MUST REMEMBER TO DO THIS NEXT TIME...!

_____
_____
_____

## INCLUDE A PHOTO, CONTACT DETAILS OF OTHER CAMPERS OR OTHER INFORMATION HERE:

# THE CAMPING Journal

TRAVEL DATE/S: _____
DEPARTURE LOCATION: _____
ARRIVAL LOCATION: _____
TOTAL MILAGE: _____ MILES/KM'S:

## WEATHER CONDITIONS ON ARRIVAL:

☀️ ⛅ 🌧️ 💨 ❄️ 🌦️

TEMP: _____

## CAMPGROUND DETAILS

NAME _____

ADDRESS _____
_____

SITE [ ]    COST [ ]    ○ DAY  ○ WEEK  ○ MONTH

FIRST VISIT ○    RETURN VISIT ○

CAMPING GROUND MANAGER [ ]

ALTERNATIVE. SITE FOR NEXT VISIT [ ]

AMENITY BLOCK PASSWORD/CODE [ ]

WIFI PASSWORD/CODE [ ]    ○ FREE  ○ FEE

CAMPING COMPANIONS OR NEW FRIENDS MET

[                              ]

CAMPSITE RATING ☆☆☆☆☆

COMMENTS
_____
_____
_____
_____
_____

### EXTRA DETAILS

**POWER**
UN-POWERED ○
POWERED ○    ○ 15 AMP  ○ 30 AMP  ○ 50 AMP

**SITE**
LEVEL ○  UN-LEVEL ○  REVERSE IN ○  PULL THROUGH ○
SUNNY ○  SHADED ○  QUIET ○  NOISY ○  VIEW ○

**AMENITIES**
TOILET ○  SHOWER ○  WATER ○  SEWER ○
CONDITION OF AMENITIES   EXCELLENT ○  GOOD ○  POOR ○

**OTHER**
CHILD FRIENDLY ○   PET FRIENDLY ○   PICNIC TABLE ○
GAMES ROOM ○   SECURITY ○   WIFI ○   T.V ○
COOKING FACILITIES ○   CAMP FIRE PERMITTED ○
HIKING ○  BEACH ○  FISHING ○  RIVER ○  LAKE ○
POOL ○  PLAYGROUND ○  SPORTS GROUND ○  GOLF ○

OTHER: _____

CONVENIENCE STORE ○         FUEL AVAILABLE ○
LAUNDRY FACILITIES ○         CAFE/RESTAURANT ○

### OTHER INFORMATION OR DETAILS
_____
_____
_____
_____
_____

# CAMPING DETAILS AND EXPERIENCES

## PLACES VISITED AND/OR ACTIVITIES COMPLETED

_____
_____
_____
_____
_____
_____
_____
_____
_____
_____

## MEMORABLE MOMENTS AND THE HIGHLIGHTS TO REMEMBER

_____
_____
_____
_____
_____
_____
_____
_____

## WE MUST REMEMBER TO DO THIS NEXT TIME...!

_____
_____
_____

## INCLUDE A PHOTO, CONTACT DETAILS OF OTHER CAMPERS OR OTHER INFORMATION HERE:

# THE CAMPING Journal

TRAVEL DATE/S: _____
DEPARTURE LOCATION: _____
ARRIVAL LOCATION: _____
TOTAL MILAGE: _____ MILES/KM'S:

### WEATHER CONDITIONS ON ARRIVAL:

TEMP: _____

## CAMPGROUND DETAILS

NAME _____
ADDRESS _____
_____

SITE [  ]   COST [  ]   DAY   WEEK   MONTH

FIRST VISIT   RETURN VISIT

CAMPING GROUND MANAGER [  ]

ALTERNATIVE. SITE FOR NEXT VISIT [  ]

AMENITY BLOCK PASSWORD/CODE [  ]

WIFI PASSWORD/CODE [  ]   FREE   FEE

CAMPING COMPANIONS OR NEW FRIENDS MET

CAMPSITE RATING ☆☆☆☆☆
COMMENTS
_____
_____
_____
_____

### EXTRA DETAILS

**POWER**
UN-POWERED
POWERED     15 AMP   30 AMP   50 AMP

**SITE**
LEVEL   UN-LEVEL   REVERSE IN   PULL THROUGH
SUNNY   SHADED   QUIET   NOISY   VIEW

**AMENITIES**
TOILET   SHOWER   WATER   SEWER
CONDITION OF AMENITIES   EXCELLENT   GOOD   POOR

**OTHER**
CHILD FRIENDLY   PET FRIENDLY   PICNIC TABLE
GAMES ROOM   SECURITY   WIFI   T.V
COOKING FACILITIES   CAMP FIRE PERMITTED
HIKING   BEACH   FISHING   RIVER   LAKE
POOL   PLAYGROUND   SPORTS GROUND   GOLF

OTHER: _____

CONVENIENCE STORE     FUEL AVAILABLE
LAUNDRY FACILITIES    CAFE/RESTAURANT

### OTHER INFORMATION OR DETAILS
_____
_____
_____
_____

# CAMPING DETAILS AND EXPERIENCES

**PLACES VISITED AND/OR ACTIVITIES COMPLETED**
_____
_____
_____
_____
_____
_____
_____
_____
_____
_____

**MEMORABLE MOMENTS AND THE HIGHLIGHTS TO REMEMBER**
_____
_____
_____
_____
_____
_____
_____
_____

**WE MUST REMEMBER TO DO THIS NEXT TIME...!**
_____
_____
_____

**INCLUDE A PHOTO, CONTACT DETAILS OF OTHER CAMPERS OR OTHER INFORMATION HERE:**

# THE CAMPING Journal

TRAVEL DATE/S: _____
DEPARTURE LOCATION: _____
ARRIVAL LOCATION: _____
TOTAL MILAGE: _____ MILES/KM'S:

## WEATHER CONDITIONS ON ARRIVAL:

TEMP: _____

## CAMPGROUND DETAILS

NAME _____

ADDRESS _____
_____

SITE [ ]   COST [ ]   DAY   WEEK   MONTH

FIRST VISIT     RETURN VISIT

CAMPING GROUND MANAGER [ ]

ALTERNATIVE. SITE FOR NEXT VISIT [ ]

AMENITY BLOCK PASSWORD/CODE [ ]

WIFI PASSWORD/CODE [ ]   FREE   FEE

CAMPING COMPANIONS OR NEW FRIENDS MET

CAMPSITE RATING ☆☆☆☆☆

COMMENTS
_____
_____
_____
_____
_____

### EXTRA DETAILS

**POWER**
UN-POWERED
POWERED     15 AMP   30 AMP   50 AMP

**SITE**
LEVEL   UN-LEVEL   REVERSE IN   PULL THROUGH
SUNNY   SHADED   QUIET   NOISY   VIEW

**AMENITIES**
TOILET   SHOWER   WATER   SEWER
CONDITION OF AMENITIES   EXCELLENT   GOOD   POOR

**OTHER**
CHILD FRIENDLY   PET FRIENDLY   PICNIC TABLE
GAMES ROOM   SECURITY   WIFI   T.V
COOKING FACILITIES   CAMP FIRE PERMITTED
HIKING   BEACH   FISHING   RIVER   LAKE
POOL   PLAYGROUND   SPORTS GROUND   GOLF
OTHER: _____
CONVENIENCE STORE     FUEL AVAILABLE
LAUNDRY FACILITIES     CAFE/RESTAURANT

### OTHER INFORMATION OR DETAILS
_____
_____
_____
_____

# CAMPING DETAILS AND EXPERIENCES

**PLACES VISITED AND/OR ACTIVITIES COMPLETED**

_____
_____
_____
_____
_____
_____
_____
_____
_____

**MEMORABLE MOMENTS AND THE HIGHLIGHTS TO REMEMBER**

_____
_____
_____
_____
_____
_____
_____
_____

**WE MUST REMEMBER TO DO THIS NEXT TIME...!**

_____
_____
_____

**INCLUDE A PHOTO, CONTACT DETAILS OF OTHER CAMPERS OR OTHER INFORMATION HERE:**

# THE CAMPING Journal

**TRAVEL DATE/S:** _____
**DEPARTURE LOCATION:** _____
**ARRIVAL LOCATION:** _____
**TOTAL MILAGE:** _____ MILES/KM'S:

**WEATHER CONDITIONS ON ARRIVAL:**

**TEMP:** _____

## CAMPGROUND DETAILS

**NAME** _____

**ADDRESS** _____
_____

**SITE** [ ]   **COST** [ ]   DAY   WEEK   MONTH

**FIRST VISIT**   **RETURN VISIT**

**CAMPING GROUND MANAGER** [ ]

**ALTERNATIVE. SITE FOR NEXT VISIT** [ ]

**AMENITY BLOCK PASSWORD/CODE** [ ]

**WIFI PASSWORD/CODE** [ ]   FREE   FEE

**CAMPING COMPANIONS OR NEW FRIENDS MET**

[ ]

**CAMPSITE RATING** ☆☆☆☆☆
**COMMENTS**
_____
_____
_____
_____

### EXTRA DETAILS

**POWER**
UN-POWERED
POWERED    15 AMP    30 AMP    50 AMP

**SITE**
LEVEL   UN-LEVEL   REVERSE IN   PULL THROUGH
SUNNY   SHADED   QUIET   NOISY   VIEW

**AMENITIES**
TOILET   SHOWER   WATER   SEWER
CONDITION OF AMENITIES   EXCELLENT   GOOD   POOR

**OTHER**
CHILD FRIENDLY   PET FRIENDLY   PICNIC TABLE
GAMES ROOM   SECURITY   WIFI   T.V
COOKING FACILITIES   CAMP FIRE PERMITTED
HIKING   BEACH   FISHING   RIVER   LAKE
POOL   PLAYGROUND   SPORTS GROUND   GOLF

OTHER: _____

CONVENIENCE STORE   FUEL AVAILABLE
LAUNDRY FACILITIES   CAFE/RESTAURANT

### OTHER INFORMATION OR DETAILS

_____
_____
_____
_____

# CAMPING DETAILS AND EXPERIENCES

## PLACES VISITED AND/OR ACTIVITIES COMPLETED

_____
_____
_____
_____
_____
_____
_____
_____
_____

## MEMORABLE MOMENTS AND THE HIGHLIGHTS TO REMEMBER

_____
_____
_____
_____
_____
_____
_____

## WE MUST REMEMBER TO DO THIS NEXT TIME...!

_____
_____
_____

## INCLUDE A PHOTO, CONTACT DETAILS OF OTHER CAMPERS OR OTHER INFORMATION HERE:

# THE CAMPING Journal

TRAVEL DATE/S: _____
DEPARTURE LOCATION: _____
ARRIVAL LOCATION: _____
TOTAL MILAGE: _____ MILES/KM'S:

**WEATHER CONDITIONS ON ARRIVAL:**

TEMP: _____

## CAMPGROUND DETAILS

NAME _____

ADDRESS _____

SITE [ ]   COST [ ]   ○ DAY  ○ WEEK  ○ MONTH

FIRST VISIT ○   RETURN VISIT ○

CAMPING GROUND MANAGER [ ]

ALTERNATIVE. SITE FOR NEXT VISIT [ ]

AMENITY BLOCK PASSWORD/CODE [ ]

WIFI PASSWORD/CODE [ ]   ○ FREE  ○ FEE

CAMPING COMPANIONS OR NEW FRIENDS MET

CAMPSITE RATING ☆☆☆☆☆

COMMENTS
_____
_____
_____
_____

### EXTRA DETAILS

**POWER**
UN-POWERED ○
POWERED ○   ○ 15 AMP   ○ 30 AMP   ○ 50 AMP

**SITE**
LEVEL ○   UN-LEVEL ○   REVERSE IN ○   PULL THROUGH ○
SUNNY ○   SHADED ○   QUIET ○   NOISY ○   VIEW ○

**AMENITIES**
TOILET ○   SHOWER ○   WATER ○   SEWER ○
CONDITION OF AMENITIES   ○ EXCELLENT   ○ GOOD   ○ POOR

**OTHER**
CHILD FRIENDLY ○   PET FRIENDLY ○   PICNIC TABLE ○
GAMES ROOM ○   SECURITY ○   WIFI ○   T.V ○
COOKING FACILITIES ○   CAMP FIRE PERMITTED ○
HIKING ○   BEACH ○   FISHING ○   RIVER ○   LAKE ○
POOL ○   PLAYGROUND ○   SPORTS GROUND ○   GOLF ○

OTHER: _____

CONVENIENCE STORE ○   FUEL AVAILABLE ○
LAUNDRY FACILITIES ○   CAFE/RESTAURANT ○

### OTHER INFORMATION OR DETAILS

_____
_____
_____
_____

# CAMPING DETAILS AND EXPERIENCES

## PLACES VISITED AND/OR ACTIVITIES COMPLETED

_____
_____
_____
_____
_____
_____
_____
_____
_____
_____
_____

## MEMORABLE MOMENTS AND THE HIGHLIGHTS TO REMEMBER

_____
_____
_____
_____
_____
_____
_____
_____
_____

## WE MUST REMEMBER TO DO THIS NEXT TIME...!

_____
_____
_____

## INCLUDE A PHOTO, CONTACT DETAILS OF OTHER CAMPERS OR OTHER INFORMATION HERE:

# THE CAMPING Journal

TRAVEL DATE/S: _____
DEPARTURE LOCATION: _____
ARRIVAL LOCATION: _____
TOTAL MILAGE: _____ MILES/KM'S:

### WEATHER CONDITIONS ON ARRIVAL:

TEMP: _____

## CAMPGROUND DETAILS

NAME _____

ADDRESS _____
_____

SITE [ ]   COST [ ]   ○ DAY  ○ WEEK  ○ MONTH

FIRST VISIT ○   RETURN VISIT ○

CAMPING GROUND MANAGER [ ]

ALTERNATIVE. SITE FOR NEXT VISIT [ ]

AMENITY BLOCK PASSWORD/CODE [ ]

WIFI PASSWORD/CODE [ ]   ○ FREE  ○ FEE

CAMPING COMPANIONS OR NEW FRIENDS MET

[                                    ]

CAMPSITE RATING ☆☆☆☆☆
COMMENTS
_____
_____
_____
_____
_____

### EXTRA DETAILS

**POWER**
UN-POWERED ○
POWERED ○   ○ 15 AMP   ○ 30 AMP   ○ 50 AMP

**SITE**
LEVEL ○   UN-LEVEL ○   REVERSE IN ○   PULL THROUGH ○
SUNNY ○   SHADED ○   QUIET ○   NOISY ○   VIEW ○

**AMENITIES**
TOILET ○   SHOWER ○   WATER ○   SEWER ○
CONDITION OF AMENITIES   EXCELLENT ○   GOOD ○   POOR ○

**OTHER**
CHILD FRIENDLY ○   PET FRIENDLY ○   PICNIC TABLE ○
GAMES ROOM ○   SECURITY ○   WIFI ○   T.V ○
COOKING FACILITIES ○   CAMP FIRE PERMITTED ○
HIKING ○   BEACH ○   FISHING ○   RIVER ○   LAKE ○
POOL ○   PLAYGROUND ○   SPORTS GROUND ○   GOLF ○

OTHER: _____

CONVENIENCE STORE ○          FUEL AVAILABLE ○
LAUNDRY FACILITIES ○          CAFE/RESTAURANT ○

### OTHER INFORMATION OR DETAILS
_____
_____
_____
_____
_____

# CAMPING DETAILS AND EXPERIENCES

## PLACES VISITED AND/OR ACTIVITIES COMPLETED

_____
_____
_____
_____
_____
_____
_____
_____
_____
_____
_____

## MEMORABLE MOMENTS AND THE HIGHLIGHTS TO REMEMBER

_____
_____
_____
_____
_____
_____
_____
_____
_____

## WE MUST REMEMBER TO DO THIS NEXT TIME...!

_____
_____
_____

## INCLUDE A PHOTO, CONTACT DETAILS OF OTHER CAMPERS OR OTHER INFORMATION HERE:

# THE CAMPING Journal

TRAVEL DATE/S: _____
DEPARTURE LOCATION: _____
ARRIVAL LOCATION: _____
TOTAL MILAGE: _____ MILES/KM'S:

**WEATHER CONDITIONS ON ARRIVAL:**

☀️ 🌤️ 🌧️ 💨 ❄️ 🌦️

TEMP: _____

## CAMPGROUND DETAILS

NAME _____

ADDRESS _____
_____

SITE [  ]    COST [  ]    DAY ○ WEEK ○ MONTH ○

FIRST VISIT ○    RETURN VISIT ○

CAMPING GROUND MANAGER [_____]

ALTERNATIVE. SITE FOR NEXT VISIT [_____]

AMENITY BLOCK PASSWORD/CODE [_____]

WIFI PASSWORD/CODE [_____]  FREE ○ FEE ○

CAMPING COMPANIONS OR NEW FRIENDS MET
[_____]

CAMPSITE RATING ☆☆☆☆☆

COMMENTS
_____
_____
_____
_____

### EXTRA DETAILS

**POWER**
UN-POWERED ○
POWERED ○   15 AMP ○   30 AMP ○   50 AMP ○

**SITE**
LEVEL ○   UN-LEVEL ○   REVERSE IN ○   PULL THROUGH ○
SUNNY ○   SHADED ○   QUIET ○   NOISY ○   VIEW ○

**AMENITIES**
TOILET ○   SHOWER ○   WATER ○   SEWER ○
CONDITION OF AMENITIES   EXCELLENT ○   GOOD ○   POOR ○

**OTHER**
CHILD FRIENDLY ○   PET FRIENDLY ○   PICNIC TABLE ○
GAMES ROOM ○   SECURITY ○   WIFI ○   T.V ○
COOKING FACILITIES ○   CAMP FIRE PERMITTED ○
HIKING ○   BEACH ○   FISHING ○   RIVER ○   LAKE ○
POOL ○   PLAYGROUND ○   SPORTS GROUND ○   GOLF ○

OTHER: _____

CONVENIENCE STORE ○          FUEL AVAILABLE ○
LAUNDRY FACILITIES ○          CAFE/RESTAURANT ○

### OTHER INFORMATION OR DETAILS
_____
_____
_____
_____

# CAMPING DETAILS AND EXPERIENCES

## PLACES VISITED AND/OR ACTIVITIES COMPLETED 🚶

_____
_____
_____
_____
_____
_____
_____
_____
_____

## MEMORABLE MOMENTS AND THE HIGHLIGHTS TO REMEMBER 👏

_____
_____
_____
_____
_____
_____
_____
_____

## WE MUST REMEMBER TO DO THIS NEXT TIME...! ✅

_____
_____
_____

**INCLUDE A PHOTO, CONTACT DETAILS OF OTHER CAMPERS OR OTHER INFORMATION HERE:**

# THE CAMPING Journal

TRAVEL DATE/S: _____
DEPARTURE LOCATION: _____
ARRIVAL LOCATION: _____
TOTAL MILAGE: _____ MILES/KM'S:

## WEATHER CONDITIONS ON ARRIVAL:

TEMP: _____

## CAMPGROUND DETAILS

NAME _____

ADDRESS _____
_____

SITE [  ]   COST [  ]   DAY   WEEK   MONTH

FIRST VISIT   RETURN VISIT

CAMPING GROUND MANAGER [         ]

ALTERNATIVE. SITE FOR NEXT VISIT [       ]

AMENITY BLOCK PASSWORD/CODE [       ]

WIFI PASSWORD/CODE [       ]   FREE   FEE

CAMPING COMPANIONS OR NEW FRIENDS MET

[                                               ]

CAMPSITE RATING ☆☆☆☆☆

COMMENTS
_____
_____
_____
_____

### EXTRA DETAILS

**POWER**
UN-POWERED
POWERED   15 AMP   30 AMP   50 AMP

**SITE**
LEVEL   UN-LEVEL   REVERSE IN   PULL THROUGH
SUNNY   SHADED   QUIET   NOISY   VIEW

**AMENITIES**
TOILET   SHOWER   WATER   SEWER
CONDITION OF AMENITIES   EXCELLENT   GOOD   POOR

**OTHER**
CHILD FRIENDLY   PET FRIENDLY   PICNIC TABLE
GAMES ROOM   SECURITY   WIFI   T.V
COOKING FACILITIES   CAMP FIRE PERMITTED
HIKING   BEACH   FISHING   RIVER   LAKE
POOL   PLAYGROUND   SPORTS GROUND   GOLF

OTHER: _____

CONVENIENCE STORE   FUEL AVAILABLE
LAUNDRY FACILITIES   CAFE/RESTAURANT

### OTHER INFORMATION OR DETAILS
_____
_____
_____
_____

# CAMPING DETAILS AND EXPERIENCES

## PLACES VISITED AND/OR ACTIVITIES COMPLETED

_____
_____
_____
_____
_____
_____
_____
_____
_____

## MEMORABLE MOMENTS AND THE HIGHLIGHTS TO REMEMBER

_____
_____
_____
_____
_____
_____
_____
_____
_____

## WE MUST REMEMBER TO DO THIS NEXT TIME...!

_____
_____
_____

## INCLUDE A PHOTO, CONTACT DETAILS OF OTHER CAMPERS OR OTHER INFORMATION HERE:

# THE CAMPING Journal

TRAVEL DATE/S: _____
DEPARTURE LOCATION: _____
ARRIVAL LOCATION: _____
TOTAL MILAGE: _____ MILES/KM'S:

### WEATHER CONDITIONS ON ARRIVAL:

TEMP: _____

## CAMPGROUND DETAILS

NAME _____

ADDRESS _____
_____

SITE [ ]   COST [ ]   DAY   WEEK   MONTH

FIRST VISIT   RETURN VISIT

CAMPING GROUND MANAGER [ ]

ALTERNATIVE. SITE FOR NEXT VISIT [ ]

AMENITY BLOCK PASSWORD/CODE [ ]

WIFI PASSWORD/CODE [ ]   FREE   FEE

CAMPING COMPANIONS OR NEW FRIENDS MET

[ ]

CAMPSITE RATING ☆☆☆☆☆

COMMENTS
_____
_____
_____
_____
_____

### EXTRA DETAILS

**POWER**
UN-POWERED
POWERED    15 AMP   30 AMP   50 AMP

**SITE**
LEVEL   UN-LEVEL   REVERSE IN   PULL THROUGH
SUNNY   SHADED   QUIET   NOISY   VIEW

**AMENITIES**
TOILET   SHOWER   WATER   SEWER
CONDITION OF AMENITIES   EXCELLENT   GOOD   POOR

**OTHER**
CHILD FRIENDLY   PET FRIENDLY   PICNIC TABLE
GAMES ROOM   SECURITY   WIFI   T.V
COOKING FACILITIES   CAMP FIRE PERMITTED
HIKING   BEACH   FISHING   RIVER   LAKE
POOL   PLAYGROUND   SPORTS GROUND   GOLF
OTHER: _____
CONVENIENCE STORE     FUEL AVAILABLE
LAUNDRY FACILITIES    CAFE/RESTAURANT

### OTHER INFORMATION OR DETAILS

_____
_____
_____
_____
_____

# CAMPING DETAILS AND EXPERIENCES

## PLACES VISITED AND/OR ACTIVITIES COMPLETED

_____
_____
_____
_____
_____
_____
_____
_____
_____
_____
_____

## MEMORABLE MOMENTS AND THE HIGHLIGHTS TO REMEMBER

_____
_____
_____
_____
_____
_____
_____
_____

## WE MUST REMEMBER TO DO THIS NEXT TIME...!

_____
_____
_____

## INCLUDE A PHOTO, CONTACT DETAILS OF OTHER CAMPERS OR OTHER INFORMATION HERE:

# THE CAMPING Journal

TRAVEL DATE/S: _____
DEPARTURE LOCATION: _____
ARRIVAL LOCATION: _____
TOTAL MILAGE: _____ MILES/KM'S:

**WEATHER CONDITIONS ON ARRIVAL:**

TEMP: _____

## CAMPGROUND DETAILS

NAME _____

ADDRESS _____

SITE [ ]    COST [ ]    DAY   WEEK   MONTH

FIRST VISIT    RETURN VISIT

CAMPING GROUND MANAGER [ ]

ALTERNATIVE. SITE FOR NEXT VISIT [ ]

AMENITY BLOCK PASSWORD/CODE [ ]

WIFI PASSWORD/CODE [ ]    FREE   FEE

CAMPING COMPANIONS OR NEW FRIENDS MET

[ ]

CAMPSITE RATING ☆☆☆☆☆
COMMENTS
_____
_____
_____
_____

### EXTRA DETAILS

**POWER**
UN-POWERED
POWERED    15 AMP   30 AMP   50 AMP

**SITE**
LEVEL   UN-LEVEL   REVERSE IN   PULL THROUGH
SUNNY   SHADED   QUIET   NOISY   VIEW

**AMENITIES**
TOILET   SHOWER   WATER   SEWER
CONDITION OF AMENITIES   EXCELLENT   GOOD   POOR

**OTHER**
CHILD FRIENDLY   PET FRIENDLY   PICNIC TABLE
GAMES ROOM   SECURITY   WIFI   T.V
COOKING FACILITIES   CAMP FIRE PERMITTED
HIKING   BEACH   FISHING   RIVER   LAKE
POOL   PLAYGROUND   SPORTS GROUND   GOLF

OTHER: _____
CONVENIENCE STORE        FUEL AVAILABLE
LAUNDRY FACILITIES        CAFE/RESTAURANT

### OTHER INFORMATION OR DETAILS
_____
_____
_____
_____

# CAMPING DETAILS AND EXPERIENCES

## PLACES VISITED AND/OR ACTIVITIES COMPLETED

_____
_____
_____
_____
_____
_____
_____
_____
_____
_____

## MEMORABLE MOMENTS AND THE HIGHLIGHTS TO REMEMBER

_____
_____
_____
_____
_____
_____
_____

## WE MUST REMEMBER TO DO THIS NEXT TIME...!

_____
_____
_____

INCLUDE A PHOTO, CONTACT DETAILS OF OTHER CAMPERS OR OTHER INFORMATION HERE:

# THE CAMPING Journal

TRAVEL DATE/S: _____
DEPARTURE LOCATION: _____
ARRIVAL LOCATION: _____
TOTAL MILAGE: _____ MILES/KM'S:

**WEATHER CONDITIONS ON ARRIVAL:**

☀️ ⛅ 🌧️ 💨 ❄️ 🌨️

TEMP: _____

## CAMPGROUND DETAILS

NAME _____

ADDRESS _____
_____

SITE [ ]   COST [ ]   DAY  WEEK  MONTH

FIRST VISIT ○   RETURN VISIT ○

CAMPING GROUND MANAGER [ ]

ALTERNATIVE. SITE FOR NEXT VISIT [ ]

AMENITY BLOCK PASSWORD/CODE [ ]

WIFI PASSWORD/CODE [ ]   FREE ○  FEE ○

CAMPING COMPANIONS OR NEW FRIENDS MET

[ ]

CAMPSITE RATING ☆☆☆☆☆

COMMENTS
_____
_____
_____
_____
_____

### EXTRA DETAILS

**POWER**
UN-POWERED ○
POWERED ○   15 AMP ○   30 AMP ○   50 AMP ○

**SITE**
LEVEL ○   UN-LEVEL ○   REVERSE IN ○   PULL THROUGH ○
SUNNY ○   SHADED ○   QUIET ○   NOISY ○   VIEW ○

**AMENITIES**
TOILET ○   SHOWER ○   WATER ○   SEWER ○
CONDITION OF AMENITIES   EXCELLENT ○   GOOD ○   POOR ○

**OTHER**
CHILD FRIENDLY ○   PET FRIENDLY ○   PICNIC TABLE ○
GAMES ROOM ○   SECURITY ○   WIFI ○   T.V ○
COOKING FACILITIES ○   CAMP FIRE PERMITTED ○
HIKING ○   BEACH ○   FISHING ○   RIVER ○   LAKE ○
POOL ○   PLAYGROUND ○   SPORTS GROUND ○   GOLF ○
OTHER: _____
CONVENIENCE STORE ○   FUEL AVAILABLE ○
LAUNDRY FACILITIES ○   CAFE/RESTAURANT ○

### OTHER INFORMATION OR DETAILS

_____
_____
_____
_____
_____

# CAMPING DETAILS AND EXPERIENCES

## PLACES VISITED AND/OR ACTIVITIES COMPLETED

_____
_____
_____
_____
_____
_____
_____
_____
_____

## MEMORABLE MOMENTS AND THE HIGHLIGHTS TO REMEMBER

_____
_____
_____
_____
_____
_____
_____
_____

## WE MUST REMEMBER TO DO THIS NEXT TIME...!

_____
_____
_____

INCLUDE A PHOTO, CONTACT DETAILS OF OTHER CAMPERS OR OTHER INFORMATION HERE:

# THE CAMPING Journal

TRAVEL DATE/S:_____
DEPARTURE LOCATION:_____
ARRIVAL LOCATION: _____
TOTAL MILAGE: _____ MILES/KM'S:

**WEATHER CONDITIONS ON ARRIVAL:**

☀️ ⛅ ⛈️ 💨 ❄️ 🌧️

TEMP: _____

## CAMPGROUND DETAILS

NAME _____

ADDRESS _____
_____

SITE [___]   COST [___]   DAY ○ WEEK ○ MONTH ○

FIRST VISIT ○   RETURN VISIT ○

CAMPING GROUND MANAGER [_____]

ALTERNATIVE. SITE FOR NEXT VISIT [_____]

AMENITY BLOCK PASSWORD/CODE [_____]

WIFI PASSWORD/CODE [_____]   FREE ○ FEE ○

CAMPING COMPANIONS OR NEW FRIENDS MET
[                                    ]

CAMPSITE RATING ☆☆☆☆☆

COMMENTS
_____
_____
_____
_____

### EXTRA DETAILS

**POWER**
UN-POWERED ○
POWERED ○    15 AMP ○   30 AMP ○   50 AMP ○

**SITE**
LEVEL ○   UN-LEVEL ○   REVERSE IN ○   PULL THROUGH ○
SUNNY ○   SHADED ○   QUIET ○   NOISY ○   VIEW ○

**AMENITIES**
TOILET ○   SHOWER ○   WATER ○   SEWER ○
CONDITION OF AMENITIES   EXCELLENT ○   GOOD ○   POOR ○

**OTHER**
CHILD FRIENDLY ○   PET FRIENDLY ○   PICNIC TABLE ○
GAMES ROOM ○   SECURITY ○   WIFI ○   T.V ○
COOKING FACILITIES ○   CAMP FIRE PERMITTED ○
HIKING ○   BEACH ○   FISHING ○   RIVER ○   LAKE ○
POOL ○   PLAYGROUND ○   SPORTS GROUND ○   GOLF ○

OTHER:_____

CONVENIENCE STORE ○        FUEL AVAILABLE ○
LAUNDRY FACILITIES ○        CAFE/RESTAURANT ○

### OTHER INFORMATION OR DETAILS
_____
_____
_____
_____

# THE CAMPING Journal

## CAMPING DETAILS AND EXPERIENCES

**PLACES VISITED AND/OR ACTIVITIES COMPLETED**

___

**MEMORABLE MOMENTS AND THE HIGHLIGHTS TO REMEMBER**

___

**WE MUST REMEMBER TO DO THIS NEXT TIME...!**

___

**INCLUDE A PHOTO, CONTACT DETAILS OF OTHER CAMPERS OR OTHER INFORMATION HERE:**

# THE CAMPING Journal

TRAVEL DATE/S: _____
DEPARTURE LOCATION: _____
ARRIVAL LOCATION: _____
TOTAL MILAGE: _____ MILES/KM'S:

## WEATHER CONDITIONS ON ARRIVAL:

TEMP: _____

## CAMPGROUND DETAILS

NAME _____

ADDRESS _____
_____

SITE [ ]    COST [ ]    DAY ○ WEEK ○ MONTH ○

FIRST VISIT ○    RETURN VISIT ○

CAMPING GROUND MANAGER [_____]

ALTERNATIVE. SITE FOR NEXT VISIT [____]

AMENITY BLOCK PASSWORD/CODE [_____]

WIFI PASSWORD/CODE [____] FREE ○ FEE ○

CAMPING COMPANIONS OR NEW FRIENDS MET

[                                    ]

CAMPSITE RATING ☆☆☆☆☆

COMMENTS
_____
_____
_____
_____

### EXTRA DETAILS

**POWER**
UN-POWERED ○
POWERED ○    15 AMP ○    30 AMP ○    50 AMP ○

**SITE**
LEVEL ○  UN-LEVEL ○  REVERSE IN ○  PULL THROUGH ○
SUNNY ○  SHADED ○  QUIET ○  NOISY ○  VIEW ○

**AMENITIES**
TOILET ○  SHOWER ○  WATER ○  SEWER ○
CONDITION OF AMENITIES  EXCELLENT ○  GOOD ○  POOR ○

**OTHER**
CHILD FRIENDLY ○  PET FRIENDLY ○  PICNIC TABLE ○
GAMES ROOM ○    SECURITY ○    WIFI ○    T.V ○
COOKING FACILITIES ○    CAMP FIRE PERMITTED ○
HIKING ○  BEACH ○  FISHING ○  RIVER ○  LAKE ○
POOL ○  PLAYGROUND ○  SPORTS GROUND ○  GOLF ○

OTHER: _____

CONVENIENCE STORE ○        FUEL AVAILABLE ○
LAUNDRY FACILITIES ○        CAFE/RESTAURANT ○

### OTHER INFORMATION OR DETAILS
_____
_____
_____
_____

# CAMPING DETAILS AND EXPERIENCES

**PLACES VISITED AND/OR ACTIVITIES COMPLETED**

_____
_____
_____
_____
_____
_____
_____
_____
_____
_____

**MEMORABLE MOMENTS AND THE HIGHLIGHTS TO REMEMBER**

_____
_____
_____
_____
_____
_____
_____
_____

**WE MUST REMEMBER TO DO THIS NEXT TIME...!**

_____
_____
_____

**INCLUDE A PHOTO, CONTACT DETAILS OF OTHER CAMPERS OR OTHER INFORMATION HERE:**

# THE CAMPING Journal

TRAVEL DATE/S: _____
DEPARTURE LOCATION: _____
ARRIVAL LOCATION: _____
TOTAL MILAGE: _____ MILES/KM'S:

**WEATHER CONDITIONS ON ARRIVAL:**

TEMP: _____

## CAMPGROUND DETAILS

NAME _____

ADDRESS _____
_____

SITE [ ]   COST [ ]   DAY   WEEK   MONTH

FIRST VISIT   RETURN VISIT

CAMPING GROUND MANAGER [ ]

ALTERNATIVE. SITE FOR NEXT VISIT [ ]

AMENITY BLOCK PASSWORD/CODE [ ]

WIFI PASSWORD/CODE [ ]   FREE   FEE

CAMPING COMPANIONS OR NEW FRIENDS MET

[ ]

CAMPSITE RATING ☆☆☆☆☆
COMMENTS
_____
_____
_____
_____

### EXTRA DETAILS

**POWER**
UN-POWERED
POWERED       15 AMP   30 AMP   50 AMP

**SITE**
LEVEL   UN-LEVEL   REVERSE IN   PULL THROUGH
SUNNY   SHADED   QUIET   NOISY   VIEW

**AMENITIES**
TOILET   SHOWER   WATER   SEWER
CONDITION OF AMENITIES   EXCELLENT   GOOD   POOR

**OTHER**
CHILD FRIENDLY   PET FRIENDLY   PICNIC TABLE
GAMES ROOM   SECURITY   WIFI   T.V
COOKING FACILITIES   CAMP FIRE PERMITTED
HIKING   BEACH   FISHING   RIVER   LAKE
POOL   PLAYGROUND   SPORTS GROUND   GOLF

OTHER: _____

CONVENIENCE STORE        FUEL AVAILABLE
LAUNDRY FACILITIES        CAFE/RESTAURANT

### OTHER INFORMATION OR DETAILS

_____
_____
_____
_____
_____

# CAMPING DETAILS AND EXPERIENCES

## PLACES VISITED AND/OR ACTIVITIES COMPLETED

_____
_____
_____
_____
_____
_____
_____
_____
_____

## MEMORABLE MOMENTS AND THE HIGHLIGHTS TO REMEMBER

_____
_____
_____
_____
_____
_____
_____

## WE MUST REMEMBER TO DO THIS NEXT TIME...!

_____
_____
_____

## INCLUDE A PHOTO, CONTACT DETAILS OF OTHER CAMPERS OR OTHER INFORMATION HERE:

# THE CAMPING Journal

TRAVEL DATE/S: _____
DEPARTURE LOCATION: _____
ARRIVAL LOCATION: _____
TOTAL MILAGE: _____ MILES/KM'S:

**WEATHER CONDITIONS ON ARRIVAL:**

☀️ ⛅ 🌧️ 💨 ❄️ 🌦️

TEMP: _____

## CAMPGROUND DETAILS

NAME _____

ADDRESS _____
_____

SITE [ ]   COST [ ]   DAY ○ WEEK ○ MONTH ○

FIRST VISIT ○   RETURN VISIT ○

CAMPING GROUND MANAGER [ ]

ALTERNATIVE. SITE FOR NEXT VISIT [ ]

AMENITY BLOCK PASSWORD/CODE [ ]

WIFI PASSWORD/CODE [ ]   FREE ○ FEE ○

CAMPING COMPANIONS OR NEW FRIENDS MET

[                                                    ]

CAMPSITE RATING ☆☆☆☆☆

COMMENTS
_____
_____
_____
_____
_____

### EXTRA DETAILS

**POWER**
UN-POWERED ○
POWERED ○   15 AMP ○   30 AMP ○   50 AMP ○

**SITE**
LEVEL ○   UN-LEVEL ○   REVERSE IN ○   PULL THROUGH ○
SUNNY ○   SHADED ○   QUIET ○   NOISY ○   VIEW ○

**AMENITIES**
TOILET ○   SHOWER ○   WATER ○   SEWER ○
CONDITION OF AMENITIES   EXCELLENT ○   GOOD ○   POOR ○

**OTHER**
CHILD FRIENDLY ○   PET FRIENDLY ○   PICNIC TABLE ○
GAMES ROOM ○   SECURITY ○   WIFI ○   T.V ○
COOKING FACILITIES ○   CAMP FIRE PERMITTED ○
HIKING ○   BEACH ○   FISHING ○   RIVER ○   LAKE ○
POOL ○   PLAYGROUND ○   SPORTS GROUND ○   GOLF ○

OTHER: _____

CONVENIENCE STORE ○   FUEL AVAILABLE ○
LAUNDRY FACILITIES ○   CAFE/RESTAURANT ○

### OTHER INFORMATION OR DETAILS

_____
_____
_____
_____
_____

# CAMPING DETAILS AND EXPERIENCES

## PLACES VISITED AND/OR ACTIVITIES COMPLETED

___

## MEMORABLE MOMENTS AND THE HIGHLIGHTS TO REMEMBER

___

## WE MUST REMEMBER TO DO THIS NEXT TIME...!

___

## INCLUDE A PHOTO, CONTACT DETAILS OF OTHER CAMPERS OR OTHER INFORMATION HERE:

# THE CAMPING Journal

TRAVEL DATE/S: _____
DEPARTURE LOCATION: _____
ARRIVAL LOCATION: _____
TOTAL MILAGE: _____ MILES/KM'S:

**WEATHER CONDITIONS ON ARRIVAL:**

TEMP: _____

## CAMPGROUND DETAILS

NAME _____

ADDRESS _____
_____

SITE [ ]   COST [ ]   DAY   WEEK   MONTH

FIRST VISIT   RETURN VISIT

CAMPING GROUND MANAGER [ ]

ALTERNATIVE. SITE FOR NEXT VISIT [ ]

AMENITY BLOCK PASSWORD/CODE [ ]

WIFI PASSWORD/CODE [ ]   FREE   FEE

**CAMPING COMPANIONS OR NEW FRIENDS MET**

CAMPSITE RATING ☆☆☆☆☆

COMMENTS
_____
_____
_____
_____

### EXTRA DETAILS

**POWER**
UN-POWERED
POWERED   15 AMP   30 AMP   50 AMP

**SITE**
LEVEL   UN-LEVEL   REVERSE IN   PULL THROUGH
SUNNY   SHADED   QUIET   NOISY   VIEW

**AMENITIES**
TOILET   SHOWER   WATER   SEWER
CONDITION OF AMENITIES   EXCELLENT   GOOD   POOR

**OTHER**
CHILD FRIENDLY   PET FRIENDLY   PICNIC TABLE
GAMES ROOM   SECURITY   WIFI   T.V
COOKING FACILITIES   CAMP FIRE PERMITTED
HIKING   BEACH   FISHING   RIVER   LAKE
POOL   PLAYGROUND   SPORTS GROUND   GOLF

OTHER: _____

CONVENIENCE STORE   FUEL AVAILABLE
LAUNDRY FACILITIES   CAFE/RESTAURANT

### OTHER INFORMATION OR DETAILS
_____
_____
_____
_____

# CAMPING DETAILS AND EXPERIENCES

**PLACES VISITED AND/OR ACTIVITIES COMPLETED**

_____
_____
_____
_____
_____
_____
_____
_____
_____

**MEMORABLE MOMENTS AND THE HIGHLIGHTS TO REMEMBER**

_____
_____
_____
_____
_____
_____
_____

**WE MUST REMEMBER TO DO THIS NEXT TIME...!**

_____
_____
_____

**INCLUDE A PHOTO, CONTACT DETAILS OF OTHER CAMPERS OR OTHER INFORMATION HERE:**

# THE CAMPING Journal

TRAVEL DATE/S: _____
DEPARTURE LOCATION: _____
ARRIVAL LOCATION: _____
TOTAL MILAGE: _____ MILES/KM'S:

**WEATHER CONDITIONS ON ARRIVAL:**

☀️ ⛅ 🌧️ 💨 ❄️ 🌦️

TEMP: _____

## CAMPGROUND DETAILS

NAME _____

ADDRESS _____
_____

SITE [ ]   COST [ ]   ○ DAY  ○ WEEK  ○ MONTH

FIRST VISIT ○   RETURN VISIT ○

CAMPING GROUND MANAGER [ ]

ALTERNATIVE. SITE FOR NEXT VISIT [ ]

AMENITY BLOCK PASSWORD/CODE [ ]

WIFI PASSWORD/CODE [ ]   ○ FREE  ○ FEE

CAMPING COMPANIONS OR NEW FRIENDS MET

[                                    ]

CAMPSITE RATING ☆☆☆☆☆

COMMENTS
_____
_____
_____
_____
_____

### EXTRA DETAILS

**POWER**
UN-POWERED ○
POWERED ○   ○ 15 AMP   ○ 30 AMP   ○ 50 AMP

**SITE**
LEVEL ○   UN-LEVEL ○   REVERSE IN ○   PULL THROUGH ○
SUNNY ○   SHADED ○   QUIET ○   NOISY ○   VIEW ○

**AMENITIES**
TOILET ○   SHOWER ○   WATER ○   SEWER ○
CONDITION OF AMENITIES   EXCELLENT ○   GOOD ○   POOR ○

**OTHER**
CHILD FRIENDLY ○   PET FRIENDLY ○   PICNIC TABLE ○
GAMES ROOM ○   SECURITY ○   WIFI ○   T.V ○
COOKING FACILITIES ○   CAMP FIRE PERMITTED ○
HIKING ○   BEACH ○   FISHING ○   RIVER ○   LAKE ○
POOL ○   PLAYGROUND ○   SPORTS GROUND ○   GOLF ○

OTHER: _____

CONVENIENCE STORE ○        FUEL AVAILABLE ○
LAUNDRY FACILITIES ○        CAFE/RESTAURANT ○

### OTHER INFORMATION OR DETAILS
_____
_____
_____
_____
_____

# CAMPING DETAILS AND EXPERIENCES

**PLACES VISITED AND/OR ACTIVITIES COMPLETED**

_____
_____
_____
_____
_____
_____
_____
_____
_____

**MEMORABLE MOMENTS AND THE HIGHLIGHTS TO REMEMBER**

_____
_____
_____
_____
_____
_____
_____
_____
_____

**WE MUST REMEMBER TO DO THIS NEXT TIME...!**

_____
_____
_____

**INCLUDE A PHOTO, CONTACT DETAILS OF OTHER CAMPERS OR OTHER INFORMATION HERE:**

# THE CAMPING Journal

TRAVEL DATE/S: _____
DEPARTURE LOCATION: _____
ARRIVAL LOCATION: _____
TOTAL MILAGE: _____ MILES/KM'S

**WEATHER CONDITIONS ON ARRIVAL:**

TEMP: _____

## CAMPGROUND DETAILS

NAME _____
ADDRESS _____
_____

SITE [ ]   COST [ ]   DAY   WEEK   MONTH
FIRST VISIT   RETURN VISIT
CAMPING GROUND MANAGER [ ]
ALTERNATIVE. SITE FOR NEXT VISIT [ ]
AMENITY BLOCK PASSWORD/CODE [ ]
WIFI PASSWORD/CODE [ ]   FREE   FEE
CAMPING COMPANIONS OR NEW FRIENDS MET

CAMPSITE RATING ☆☆☆☆☆
COMMENTS
_____
_____
_____
_____

### EXTRA DETAILS

**POWER**
UN-POWERED
POWERED   15 AMP   30 AMP   50 AMP

**SITE**
LEVEL   UN-LEVEL   REVERSE IN   PULL THROUGH
SUNNY   SHADED   QUIET   NOISY   VIEW

**AMENITIES**
TOILET   SHOWER   WATER   SEWER
CONDITION OF AMENITIES   EXCELLENT   GOOD   POOR

**OTHER**
CHILD FRIENDLY   PET FRIENDLY   PICNIC TABLE
GAMES ROOM   SECURITY   WIFI   T.V
COOKING FACILITIES   CAMP FIRE PERMITTED
HIKING   BEACH   FISHING   RIVER   LAKE
POOL   PLAYGROUND   SPORTS GROUND   GOLF

OTHER: _____
CONVENIENCE STORE   FUEL AVAILABLE
LAUNDRY FACILITIES   CAFE/RESTAURANT

### OTHER INFORMATION OR DETAILS
_____
_____
_____
_____
_____

# THE CAMPING Journal

# CAMPING DETAILS AND EXPERIENCES
× × × × × × × × × × × × × × × × × × × × × × × ×

## PLACES VISITED AND/OR ACTIVITIES COMPLETED

___

## MEMORABLE MOMENTS AND THE HIGHLIGHTS TO REMEMBER

___

## WE MUST REMEMBER TO DO THIS NEXT TIME...!

___

## INCLUDE A PHOTO, CONTACT DETAILS OF OTHER CAMPERS OR OTHER INFORMATION HERE:

# THE CAMPING Journal

TRAVEL DATE/S: _____
DEPARTURE LOCATION: _____
ARRIVAL LOCATION: _____
TOTAL MILAGE: _____ MILES/KM'S:

**WEATHER CONDITIONS ON ARRIVAL:**

TEMP: _____

## CAMPGROUND DETAILS

NAME _____

ADDRESS _____
_____

SITE [   ]   COST [   ]   DAY ○ WEEK ○ MONTH ○

FIRST VISIT ○   RETURN VISIT ○

CAMPING GROUND MANAGER [   ]

ALTERNATIVE. SITE FOR NEXT VISIT [   ]

AMENITY BLOCK PASSWORD/CODE [   ]

WIFI PASSWORD/CODE [   ]   FREE ○ FEE ○

CAMPING COMPANIONS OR NEW FRIENDS MET

CAMPSITE RATING ☆☆☆☆☆

COMMENTS
_____
_____
_____
_____
_____

### EXTRA DETAILS

**POWER**
UN-POWERED ○
POWERED ○   15 AMP ○   30 AMP ○   50 AMP ○

**SITE**
LEVEL ○   UN-LEVEL ○   REVERSE IN ○   PULL THROUGH ○
SUNNY ○   SHADED ○   QUIET ○   NOISY ○   VIEW ○

**AMENITIES**
TOILET ○   SHOWER ○   WATER ○   SEWER ○
CONDITION OF AMENITIES   EXCELLENT ○   GOOD ○   POOR ○

**OTHER**
CHILD FRIENDLY ○   PET FRIENDLY ○   PICNIC TABLE ○
GAMES ROOM ○   SECURITY ○   WIFI ○   T.V ○
COOKING FACILITIES ○   CAMP FIRE PERMITTED ○
HIKING ○   BEACH ○   FISHING ○   RIVER ○   LAKE ○
POOL ○   PLAYGROUND ○   SPORTS GROUND ○   GOLF ○

OTHER: _____

CONVENIENCE STORE ○     FUEL AVAILABLE ○
LAUNDRY FACILITIES ○     CAFE/RESTAURANT ○

### OTHER INFORMATION OR DETAILS
_____
_____
_____
_____

# CAMPING DETAILS AND EXPERIENCES

**PLACES VISITED AND/OR ACTIVITIES COMPLETED**

_____
_____
_____
_____
_____
_____
_____
_____

**MEMORABLE MOMENTS AND THE HIGHLIGHTS TO REMEMBER**

_____
_____
_____
_____
_____
_____
_____

**WE MUST REMEMBER TO DO THIS NEXT TIME...!**

_____
_____

**INCLUDE A PHOTO, CONTACT DETAILS OF OTHER CAMPERS OR OTHER INFORMATION HERE:**

# THE CAMPING Journal

TRAVEL DATE/S:_____
DEPARTURE LOCATION:_____
ARRIVAL LOCATION: _____
TOTAL MILAGE: _____ MILES/KM'S:

**WEATHER CONDITIONS ON ARRIVAL:**

☀️ ⛅ ⛈️ 💨 ❄️ 🌦️

TEMP: _____

## CAMPGROUND DETAILS

NAME_____

ADDRESS_____
_____

SITE [   ]   COST [   ]   DAY ○ WEEK ○ MONTH ○

FIRST VISIT ○   RETURN VISIT ○

CAMPING GROUND MANAGER [          ]

ALTERNATIVE. SITE FOR NEXT VISIT [     ]

AMENITY BLOCK PASSWORD/CODE [       ]

WIFI PASSWORD/CODE [     ]   FREE ○ FEE ○

CAMPING COMPANIONS OR NEW FRIENDS MET

[                                                ]

CAMPSITE RATING ☆☆☆☆☆
COMMENTS
_____
_____
_____
_____

### EXTRA DETAILS

**POWER**
UN-POWERED ○
POWERED ○   15 AMP ○   30 AMP ○   50 AMP ○

**SITE**
LEVEL ○   UN-LEVEL ○   REVERSE IN ○   PULL THROUGH ○
SUNNY ○   SHADED ○   QUIET ○   NOISY ○   VIEW ○

**AMENITIES**
TOILET ○   SHOWER ○   WATER ○   SEWER ○
CONDITION OF AMENITIES   EXCELLENT ○   GOOD ○   POOR ○

**OTHER**
CHILD FRIENDLY ○   PET FRIENDLY ○   PICNIC TABLE ○
GAMES ROOM ○   SECURITY ○   WIFI ○   T.V ○
COOKING FACILITIES ○   CAMP FIRE PERMITTED ○
HIKING ○   BEACH ○   FISHING ○   RIVER ○   LAKE ○
POOL ○   PLAYGROUND ○   SPORTS GROUND ○   GOLF ○

OTHER:_____

CONVENIENCE STORE ○   FUEL AVAILABLE ○
LAUNDRY FACILITIES ○   CAFE/RESTAURANT ○

### OTHER INFORMATION OR DETAILS

_____
_____
_____
_____
_____

# THE CAMPING Journal

# CAMPING DETAILS AND EXPERIENCES

## PLACES VISITED AND/OR ACTIVITIES COMPLETED

_____
_____
_____
_____
_____
_____
_____
_____
_____
_____

## MEMORABLE MOMENTS AND THE HIGHLIGHTS TO REMEMBER

_____
_____
_____
_____
_____
_____
_____
_____

## WE MUST REMEMBER TO DO THIS NEXT TIME...!

_____
_____
_____

## INCLUDE A PHOTO, CONTACT DETAILS OF OTHER CAMPERS OR OTHER INFORMATION HERE:

# THE CAMPING Journal

TRAVEL DATE/S: _____
DEPARTURE LOCATION: _____
ARRIVAL LOCATION: _____
TOTAL MILAGE: _____ MILES/KM'S:

## WEATHER CONDITIONS ON ARRIVAL:

TEMP: _____

## CAMPGROUND DETAILS

NAME _____

ADDRESS _____
_____

SITE [___]  COST [___]  DAY ○ WEEK ○ MONTH ○

FIRST VISIT ○   RETURN VISIT ○

CAMPING GROUND MANAGER [_____]

ALTERNATIVE. SITE FOR NEXT VISIT [_____]

AMENITY BLOCK PASSWORD/CODE [_____]

WIFI PASSWORD/CODE [_____]  FREE ○ FEE ○

CAMPING COMPANIONS OR NEW FRIENDS MET

CAMPSITE RATING ☆☆☆☆☆

COMMENTS
_____
_____
_____
_____
_____

## EXTRA DETAILS

**POWER**
UN-POWERED ○
POWERED ○   15 AMP ○   30 AMP ○   50 AMP ○

**SITE**
LEVEL ○   UN-LEVEL ○   REVERSE IN ○   PULL THROUGH ○
SUNNY ○   SHADED ○   QUIET ○   NOISY ○   VIEW ○

**AMENITIES**
TOILET ○   SHOWER ○   WATER ○   SEWER ○
CONDITION OF AMENITIES   EXCELLENT ○   GOOD ○   POOR ○

**OTHER**
CHILD FRIENDLY ○   PET FRIENDLY ○   PICNIC TABLE ○
GAMES ROOM ○   SECURITY ○   WIFI ○   T.V ○
COOKING FACILITIES ○   CAMP FIRE PERMITTED ○
HIKING ○   BEACH ○   FISHING ○   RIVER ○   LAKE ○
POOL ○   PLAYGROUND ○   SPORTS GROUND ○   GOLF ○
OTHER: _____
CONVENIENCE STORE ○   FUEL AVAILABLE ○
LAUNDRY FACILITIES ○   CAFE/RESTAURANT ○

## OTHER INFORMATION OR DETAILS

_____
_____
_____
_____
_____

# CAMPING DETAILS AND EXPERIENCES

## PLACES VISITED AND/OR ACTIVITIES COMPLETED 🚶

_____
_____
_____
_____
_____
_____
_____
_____
_____

## MEMORABLE MOMENTS AND THE HIGHLIGHTS TO REMEMBER 👏

_____
_____
_____
_____
_____
_____
_____
_____

## WE MUST REMEMBER TO DO THIS NEXT TIME…! ☑

_____
_____
_____

## INCLUDE A PHOTO, CONTACT DETAILS OF OTHER CAMPERS OR OTHER INFORMATION HERE:

# THE CAMPING Journal

TRAVEL DATE/S: _____
DEPARTURE LOCATION: _____
ARRIVAL LOCATION: _____
TOTAL MILAGE: _____ MILES/KM'S:

## WEATHER CONDITIONS ON ARRIVAL:

TEMP: _____

## CAMPGROUND DETAILS

NAME _____

ADDRESS _____
_____

SITE [ ]   COST [ ]   DAY   WEEK   MONTH

FIRST VISIT   RETURN VISIT

CAMPING GROUND MANAGER [ ]

ALTERNATIVE. SITE FOR NEXT VISIT [ ]

AMENITY BLOCK PASSWORD/CODE [ ]

WIFI PASSWORD/CODE [ ]   FREE   FEE

CAMPING COMPANIONS OR NEW FRIENDS MET

[ ]

CAMPSITE RATING ☆☆☆☆☆
COMMENTS
_____
_____
_____
_____

### EXTRA DETAILS

**POWER**
UN-POWERED
POWERED   15 AMP   30 AMP   50 AMP

**SITE**
LEVEL   UN-LEVEL   REVERSE IN   PULL THROUGH
SUNNY   SHADED   QUIET   NOISY   VIEW

**AMENITIES**
TOILET   SHOWER   WATER   SEWER
CONDITION OF AMENITIES   EXCELLENT   GOOD   POOR

**OTHER**
CHILD FRIENDLY   PET FRIENDLY   PICNIC TABLE
GAMES ROOM   SECURITY   WIFI   T.V
COOKING FACILITIES   CAMP FIRE PERMITTED
HIKING   BEACH   FISHING   RIVER   LAKE
POOL   PLAYGROUND   SPORTS GROUND   GOLF

OTHER: _____
CONVENIENCE STORE   FUEL AVAILABLE
LAUNDRY FACILITIES   CAFE/RESTAURANT

### OTHER INFORMATION OR DETAILS
_____
_____
_____
_____

# THE CAMPING Journal

# CAMPING DETAILS AND EXPERIENCES

**PLACES VISITED AND/OR ACTIVITIES COMPLETED**

_____
_____
_____
_____
_____
_____
_____
_____
_____

**MEMORABLE MOMENTS AND THE HIGHLIGHTS TO REMEMBER**

_____
_____
_____
_____
_____
_____
_____
_____
_____

**WE MUST REMEMBER TO DO THIS NEXT TIME...!**

_____
_____
_____

**INCLUDE A PHOTO, CONTACT DETAILS OF OTHER CAMPERS OR OTHER INFORMATION HERE:**

# THE CAMPING Journal

TRAVEL DATE/S:_____
DEPARTURE LOCATION:_____
ARRIVAL LOCATION:_____
TOTAL MILAGE:_____ MILES/KM'S:

## WEATHER CONDITIONS ON ARRIVAL:

TEMP:_____

## CAMPGROUND DETAILS

NAME_____

ADDRESS_____

SITE [ ]   COST [ ]   DAY   WEEK   MONTH

FIRST VISIT    RETURN VISIT

CAMPING GROUND MANAGER [ ]

ALTERNATIVE. SITE FOR NEXT VISIT [ ]

AMENITY BLOCK PASSWORD/CODE [ ]

WIFI PASSWORD/CODE [ ]   FREE   FEE

CAMPING COMPANIONS OR NEW FRIENDS MET

CAMPSITE RATING ☆☆☆☆☆

COMMENTS
_____
_____
_____
_____

### EXTRA DETAILS

**POWER**
UN-POWERED
POWERED    15 AMP    30 AMP    50 AMP

**SITE**
LEVEL   UN-LEVEL   REVERSE IN   PULL THROUGH
SUNNY   SHADED   QUIET   NOISY   VIEW

**AMENITIES**
TOILET   SHOWER   WATER   SEWER
CONDITION OF AMENITIES   EXCELLENT   GOOD   POOR

**OTHER**
CHILD FRIENDLY   PET FRIENDLY   PICNIC TABLE
GAMES ROOM   SECURITY   WIFI   T.V
COOKING FACILITIES   CAMP FIRE PERMITTED
HIKING   BEACH   FISHING   RIVER   LAKE
POOL   PLAYGROUND   SPORTS GROUND   GOLF

OTHER:_____
CONVENIENCE STORE          FUEL AVAILABLE
LAUNDRY FACILITIES          CAFE/RESTAURANT

### OTHER INFORMATION OR DETAILS
_____
_____
_____
_____

# CAMPING DETAILS AND EXPERIENCES

## PLACES VISITED AND/OR ACTIVITIES COMPLETED

___

## MEMORABLE MOMENTS AND THE HIGHLIGHTS TO REMEMBER

___

## WE MUST REMEMBER TO DO THIS NEXT TIME...!

___

**INCLUDE A PHOTO, CONTACT DETAILS OF OTHER CAMPERS OR OTHER INFORMATION HERE:**

# THE CAMPING Journal

TRAVEL DATE/S: _____
DEPARTURE LOCATION: _____
ARRIVAL LOCATION: _____
TOTAL MILAGE: _____ MILES/KM'S:

**WEATHER CONDITIONS ON ARRIVAL:**

☀️ ⛅ 🌧️ 💨 ❄️ 🌦️

TEMP: _____

## CAMPGROUND DETAILS

NAME _____

ADDRESS _____
_____

SITE [ ]   COST [ ]   DAY ○   WEEK ○   MONTH ○

FIRST VISIT ○   RETURN VISIT ○

CAMPING GROUND MANAGER [ ]

ALTERNATIVE. SITE FOR NEXT VISIT [ ]

AMENITY BLOCK PASSWORD/CODE [ ]

WIFI PASSWORD/CODE [ ]   FREE ○   FEE ○

CAMPING COMPANIONS OR NEW FRIENDS MET

[ ]

CAMPSITE RATING ☆☆☆☆☆

COMMENTS
_____
_____
_____
_____
_____

### EXTRA DETAILS

**POWER**
UN-POWERED ○
POWERED ○   15 AMP ○   30 AMP ○   50 AMP ○

**SITE**
LEVEL ○   UN-LEVEL ○   REVERSE IN ○   PULL THROUGH ○
SUNNY ○   SHADED ○   QUIET ○   NOISY ○   VIEW ○

**AMENITIES**
TOILET ○   SHOWER ○   WATER ○   SEWER ○
CONDITION OF AMENITIES   EXCELLENT ○   GOOD ○   POOR ○

**OTHER**
CHILD FRIENDLY ○   PET FRIENDLY ○   PICNIC TABLE ○
GAMES ROOM ○   SECURITY ○   WIFI ○   T.V ○
COOKING FACILITIES ○   CAMP FIRE PERMITTED ○
HIKING ○   BEACH ○   FISHING ○   RIVER ○   LAKE ○
POOL ○   PLAYGROUND ○   SPORTS GROUND ○   GOLF ○

OTHER: _____

CONVENIENCE STORE ○   FUEL AVAILABLE ○
LAUNDRY FACILITIES ○   CAFE/RESTAURANT ○

### OTHER INFORMATION OR DETAILS

_____
_____
_____
_____
_____

# THE CAMPING Journal

## CAMPING DETAILS AND EXPERIENCES

**PLACES VISITED AND/OR ACTIVITIES COMPLETED**

___

**MEMORABLE MOMENTS AND THE HIGHLIGHTS TO REMEMBER**

___

**WE MUST REMEMBER TO DO THIS NEXT TIME...!**

___

**INCLUDE A PHOTO, CONTACT DETAILS OF OTHER CAMPERS OR OTHER INFORMATION HERE:**

# THE CAMPING Journal

TRAVEL DATE/S: _____
DEPARTURE LOCATION: _____
ARRIVAL LOCATION: _____
TOTAL MILAGE: _____ MILES/KM'S:

**WEATHER CONDITIONS ON ARRIVAL:**

TEMP: _____

## CAMPGROUND DETAILS

NAME _____

ADDRESS _____

SITE [ ]    COST [ ]    DAY    WEEK    MONTH

FIRST VISIT    RETURN VISIT

CAMPING GROUND MANAGER [ ]

ALTERNATIVE. SITE FOR NEXT VISIT [ ]

AMENITY BLOCK PASSWORD/CODE [ ]

WIFI PASSWORD/CODE [ ]    FREE    FEE

CAMPING COMPANIONS OR NEW FRIENDS MET

CAMPSITE RATING ☆☆☆☆☆

COMMENTS
_____
_____
_____
_____
_____

### EXTRA DETAILS

**POWER**
UN-POWERED
POWERED    15 AMP    30 AMP    50 AMP

**SITE**
LEVEL    UN-LEVEL    REVERSE IN    PULL THROUGH
SUNNY    SHADED    QUIET    NOISY    VIEW

**AMENITIES**
TOILET    SHOWER    WATER    SEWER
CONDITION OF AMENITIES    EXCELLENT    GOOD    POOR

**OTHER**
CHILD FRIENDLY    PET FRIENDLY    PICNIC TABLE
GAMES ROOM    SECURITY    WIFI    T.V
COOKING FACILITIES    CAMP FIRE PERMITTED
HIKING    BEACH    FISHING    RIVER    LAKE
POOL    PLAYGROUND    SPORTS GROUND    GOLF

OTHER: _____

CONVENIENCE STORE    FUEL AVAILABLE
LAUNDRY FACILITIES    CAFE/RESTAURANT

### OTHER INFORMATION OR DETAILS
_____
_____
_____
_____

# CAMPING DETAILS AND EXPERIENCES

## PLACES VISITED AND/OR ACTIVITIES COMPLETED

_____
_____
_____
_____
_____
_____
_____
_____
_____
_____
_____
_____

## MEMORABLE MOMENTS AND THE HIGHLIGHTS TO REMEMBER

_____
_____
_____
_____
_____
_____
_____
_____
_____

## WE MUST REMEMBER TO DO THIS NEXT TIME...!

_____
_____
_____

## INCLUDE A PHOTO, CONTACT DETAILS OF OTHER CAMPERS OR OTHER INFORMATION HERE:

# THE CAMPING Journal

TRAVEL DATE/S:_____
DEPARTURE LOCATION:_____
ARRIVAL LOCATION: _____
TOTAL MILAGE: _____ MILES/KM'S:

## WEATHER CONDITIONS ON ARRIVAL:

TEMP: _____

## CAMPGROUND DETAILS

NAME_____

ADDRESS_____
_____

SITE [　] COST [　] DAY ○ WEEK ○ MONTH ○

FIRST VISIT ○  RETURN VISIT ○

CAMPING GROUND MANAGER [　　　　]

ALTERNATIVE. SITE FOR NEXT VISIT [　　]

AMENITY BLOCK PASSWORD/CODE [　　　]

WIFI PASSWORD/CODE [　　　] FREE ○ FEE ○

CAMPING COMPANIONS OR NEW FRIENDS MET

CAMPSITE RATING ☆☆☆☆☆
COMMENTS
_____
_____
_____
_____
_____

### EXTRA DETAILS

**POWER**
UN-POWERED ○
POWERED ○    15 AMP ○   30 AMP ○   50 AMP ○

**SITE**
LEVEL ○  UN-LEVEL ○  REVERSE IN ○  PULL THROUGH ○
SUNNY ○  SHADED ○  QUIET ○  NOISY ○  VIEW ○

**AMENITIES**
TOILET ○  SHOWER ○  WATER ○  SEWER ○
CONDITION OF AMENITIES  EXCELLENT ○  GOOD ○  POOR ○

**OTHER**
CHILD FRIENDLY ○  PET FRIENDLY ○  PICNIC TABLE ○
GAMES ROOM ○  SECURITY ○  WIFI ○  T.V ○
COOKING FACILITIES ○  CAMP FIRE PERMITTED ○
HIKING ○  BEACH ○  FISHING ○  RIVER ○  LAKE ○
POOL ○  PLAYGROUND ○  SPORTS GROUND ○  GOLF ○
OTHER:_____
CONVENIENCE STORE ○  FUEL AVAILABLE ○
LAUNDRY FACILITIES ○  CAFE/RESTAURANT ○

### OTHER INFORMATION OR DETAILS
_____
_____
_____
_____
_____

# CAMPING DETAILS AND EXPERIENCES

## PLACES VISITED AND/OR ACTIVITIES COMPLETED

## MEMORABLE MOMENTS AND THE HIGHLIGHTS TO REMEMBER

## WE MUST REMEMBER TO DO THIS NEXT TIME...!

## INCLUDE A PHOTO, CONTACT DETAILS OF OTHER CAMPERS OR OTHER INFORMATION HERE:

# THE CAMPING Journal

TRAVEL DATE/S: _____
DEPARTURE LOCATION: _____
ARRIVAL LOCATION: _____
TOTAL MILAGE: _____ MILES/KM'S:

## WEATHER CONDITIONS ON ARRIVAL:

☀️ ⛅ 🌧️ 💨 ❄️ 🌦️

TEMP: _____

## CAMPGROUND DETAILS

NAME _____

ADDRESS _____
_____

SITE [ ]   COST [ ]   DAY ○   WEEK ○   MONTH ○

FIRST VISIT ○   RETURN VISIT ○

CAMPING GROUND MANAGER [ ]

ALTERNATIVE. SITE FOR NEXT VISIT [ ]

AMENITY BLOCK PASSWORD/CODE [ ]

WIFI PASSWORD/CODE [ ]   FREE ○   FEE ○

CAMPING COMPANIONS OR NEW FRIENDS MET

[                                        ]

CAMPSITE RATING ☆☆☆☆☆

COMMENTS
_____
_____
_____
_____
_____

### EXTRA DETAILS

**POWER**
UN-POWERED ○
POWERED ○   15 AMP ○   30 AMP ○   50 AMP ○

**SITE**
LEVEL ○   UN-LEVEL ○   REVERSE IN ○   PULL THROUGH ○
SUNNY ○   SHADED ○   QUIET ○   NOISY ○   VIEW ○

**AMENITIES**
TOILET ○   SHOWER ○   WATER ○   SEWER ○
CONDITION OF AMENITIES   EXCELLENT ○   GOOD ○   POOR ○

**OTHER**
CHILD FRIENDLY ○   PET FRIENDLY ○   PICNIC TABLE ○
GAMES ROOM ○   SECURITY ○   WIFI ○   T.V ○
COOKING FACILITIES ○   CAMP FIRE PERMITTED ○
HIKING ○   BEACH ○   FISHING ○   RIVER ○   LAKE ○
POOL ○   PLAYGROUND ○   SPORTS GROUND ○   GOLF ○

OTHER: _____

CONVENIENCE STORE ○   FUEL AVAILABLE ○
LAUNDRY FACILITIES ○   CAFE/RESTAURANT ○

### OTHER INFORMATION OR DETAILS
_____
_____
_____
_____
_____

# CAMPING DETAILS AND EXPERIENCES

**PLACES VISITED AND/OR ACTIVITIES COMPLETED**

_____
_____
_____
_____
_____
_____
_____
_____
_____

**MEMORABLE MOMENTS AND THE HIGHLIGHTS TO REMEMBER**

_____
_____
_____
_____
_____
_____
_____
_____

**WE MUST REMEMBER TO DO THIS NEXT TIME...!**

_____
_____

**INCLUDE A PHOTO, CONTACT DETAILS OF OTHER CAMPERS OR OTHER INFORMATION HERE:**

# THE CAMPING Journal

TRAVEL DATE/S: _____
DEPARTURE LOCATION: _____
ARRIVAL LOCATION: _____
TOTAL MILAGE: _____ MILES/KM'S:

**WEATHER CONDITIONS ON ARRIVAL:**

TEMP: _____

## CAMPGROUND DETAILS

NAME _____

ADDRESS _____
_____

SITE [ ]  COST [ ]  DAY  WEEK  MONTH

FIRST VISIT  RETURN VISIT

CAMPING GROUND MANAGER [ ]

ALTERNATIVE. SITE FOR NEXT VISIT [ ]

AMENITY BLOCK PASSWORD/CODE [ ]

WIFI PASSWORD/CODE [ ]  FREE  FEE

**CAMPING COMPANIONS OR NEW FRIENDS MET**

CAMPSITE RATING ☆☆☆☆☆
COMMENTS
_____
_____
_____
_____
_____

### EXTRA DETAILS

**POWER**
UN-POWERED
POWERED    15 AMP   30 AMP   50 AMP

**SITE**
LEVEL   UN-LEVEL   REVERSE IN   PULL THROUGH
SUNNY   SHADED   QUIET   NOISY   VIEW

**AMENITIES**
TOILET   SHOWER   WATER   SEWER
CONDITION OF AMENITIES   EXCELLENT   GOOD   POOR

**OTHER**
CHILD FRIENDLY   PET FRIENDLY   PICNIC TABLE
GAMES ROOM   SECURITY   WIFI   T.V
COOKING FACILITIES   CAMP FIRE PERMITTED
HIKING   BEACH   FISHING   RIVER   LAKE
POOL   PLAYGROUND   SPORTS GROUND   GOLF

OTHER: _____
CONVENIENCE STORE      FUEL AVAILABLE
LAUNDRY FACILITIES      CAFE/RESTAURANT

### OTHER INFORMATION OR DETAILS
_____
_____
_____
_____
_____

# CAMPING DETAILS AND EXPERIENCES

**PLACES VISITED AND/OR ACTIVITIES COMPLETED**

_____
_____
_____
_____
_____
_____
_____
_____
_____
_____

**MEMORABLE MOMENTS AND THE HIGHLIGHTS TO REMEMBER**

_____
_____
_____
_____
_____
_____
_____
_____

**WE MUST REMEMBER TO DO THIS NEXT TIME...!**

_____
_____
_____

**INCLUDE A PHOTO, CONTACT DETAILS OF OTHER CAMPERS OR OTHER INFORMATION HERE:**

# THE CAMPING Journal

TRAVEL DATE/S: _____
DEPARTURE LOCATION: _____
ARRIVAL LOCATION: _____
TOTAL MILAGE: _____ MILES/KM'S:

**WEATHER CONDITIONS ON ARRIVAL:**

☀️ ⛅ 🌧️ 💨 ❄️ 🌦️

TEMP: _____

## CAMPGROUND DETAILS

NAME _____

ADDRESS _____
_____

SITE [   ]   COST [   ]   DAY ○  WEEK ○  MONTH ○

FIRST VISIT ○   RETURN VISIT ○

CAMPING GROUND MANAGER [_____]

ALTERNATIVE. SITE FOR NEXT VISIT [_____]

AMENITY BLOCK PASSWORD/CODE [_____]

WIFI PASSWORD/CODE [_____]  FREE ○  FEE ○

CAMPING COMPANIONS OR NEW FRIENDS MET

[                                    ]

CAMPSITE RATING ☆☆☆☆☆

COMMENTS
_____
_____
_____
_____

### EXTRA DETAILS

**POWER**
UN-POWERED ○
POWERED ○   15 AMP ○   30 AMP ○   50 AMP ○

**SITE**
LEVEL ○   UN-LEVEL ○   REVERSE IN ○   PULL THROUGH ○
SUNNY ○   SHADED ○   QUIET ○   NOISY ○   VIEW ○

**AMENITIES**
TOILET ○   SHOWER ○   WATER ○   SEWER ○
CONDITION OF AMENITIES   EXCELLENT ○   GOOD ○   POOR ○

**OTHER**
CHILD FRIENDLY ○   PET FRIENDLY ○   PICNIC TABLE ○
GAMES ROOM ○   SECURITY ○   WIFI ○   T.V ○
COOKING FACILITIES ○   CAMP FIRE PERMITTED ○
HIKING ○   BEACH ○   FISHING ○   RIVER ○   LAKE ○
POOL ○   PLAYGROUND ○   SPORTS GROUND ○   GOLF ○

OTHER: _____

CONVENIENCE STORE ○        FUEL AVAILABLE ○
LAUNDRY FACILITIES ○        CAFE/RESTAURANT ○

### OTHER INFORMATION OR DETAILS
_____
_____
_____
_____
_____

# CAMPING DETAILS AND EXPERIENCES

## PLACES VISITED AND/OR ACTIVITIES COMPLETED 🥾

_____
_____
_____
_____
_____
_____
_____
_____
_____
_____

## MEMORABLE MOMENTS AND THE HIGHLIGHTS TO REMEMBER 👏

_____
_____
_____
_____
_____
_____
_____
_____
_____

## WE MUST REMEMBER TO DO THIS NEXT TIME...! ✅

_____
_____
_____

## INCLUDE A PHOTO, CONTACT DETAILS OF OTHER CAMPERS OR OTHER INFORMATION HERE:

# CONTACT DETAILS

**CONTACT DETAILS OF NEW FRIENDS OR FELLOW CAMPERS**

NAME
PHONE
EMAIL
OTHER

NAME
PHONE
EMAIL
OTHER

NAME
PHONE
EMAIL
OTHER

NAME
PHONE
EMAIL
OTHER

NAME
PHONE
EMAIL
OTHER

# CONTACT DETAILS

## CONTACT DETAILS OF NEW FRIENDS OR FELLOW CAMPERS

**NAME**
_____
**PHONE**
_____
**EMAIL**
_____
**OTHER**
_____

**NAME**
_____
**PHONE**
_____
**EMAIL**
_____
**OTHER**
_____

**NAME**
_____
**PHONE**
_____
**EMAIL**
_____
**OTHER**
_____

**NAME**
_____
**PHONE**
_____
**EMAIL**
_____
**OTHER**
_____

**NAME**
_____
**PHONE**
_____
**EMAIL**
_____
**OTHER**
_____

# CONTACT DETAILS

**CONTACT DETAILS OF NEW FRIENDS OR FELLOW CAMPERS**

NAME
PHONE
EMAIL
OTHER

NAME
PHONE
EMAIL
OTHER

NAME
PHONE
EMAIL
OTHER

NAME
PHONE
EMAIL
OTHER

NAME
PHONE
EMAIL
OTHER

# CONTACT DETAILS

**CONTACT DETAILS OF NEW FRIENDS OR FELLOW CAMPERS**

NAME
_____
PHONE
_____
EMAIL
_____
OTHER
_____

NAME
_____
PHONE
_____
EMAIL
_____
OTHER
_____

NAME
_____
PHONE
_____
EMAIL
_____
OTHER
_____

NAME
_____
PHONE
_____
EMAIL
_____
OTHER
_____

NAME
_____
PHONE
_____
EMAIL
_____
OTHER
_____

# PHOTOS

PHOTO COLLECTION OF MEMORABLE MOMENTS

# PHOTOS

PHOTO COLLECTION OF MEMORABLE MOMENTS

# PHOTOS

**PHOTO COLLECTION OF MEMORABLE MOMENTS**

# PHOTOS

PHOTO COLLECTION OF MEMORABLE MOMENTS

# MAINTENANCE LOG

DATE SERVICED: _____

SERVICE REPAIR CENTRE NAME: _____

LOCATION: _____

VEHICLE MILAGE AT TIME OF SERVICE: [ MILES/KM'S ]   COST OF SERVICE: [    ]

PARTICULARS/DETAILS OF SERVICE:

_____

_____

_____

NEXT SERVICE DUE? [                    ]

- - - - - - - - - - - - - - - - - - - - - - - - - - - - - - - - - - - - - - - -

DATE SERVICED: _____

SERVICE REPAIR CENTRE NAME: _____

LOCATION: _____

VEHICLE MILAGE AT TIME OF SERVICE: [ MILES/KM'S ]   COST OF SERVICE: [    ]

PARTICULARS/DETAILS OF SERVICE:

_____

_____

_____

NEXT SERVICE DUE? [                    ]

# MAINTENANCE LOG

DATE SERVICED: _____

SERVICE REPAIR CENTRE NAME: _____

LOCATION: _____

VEHICLE MILAGE AT TIME OF SERVICE: [_____] MILES/KM'S    COST OF SERVICE: [_____]

PARTICULARS/DETAILS OF SERVICE:

_____

_____

_____

NEXT SERVICE DUE? [_____]

- - - - - - - - - - - - - - - - - - - - - - - - - - - - - - - - - - - - - - - -

DATE SERVICED: _____

SERVICE REPAIR CENTRE NAME: _____

LOCATION: _____

VEHICLE MILAGE AT TIME OF SERVICE: [_____] MILES/KM'S    COST OF SERVICE: [_____]

PARTICULARS/DETAILS OF SERVICE:

_____

_____

_____

NEXT SERVICE DUE? [_____]

# MAINTENANCE LOG

DATE SERVICED: _____

SERVICE REPAIR CENTRE NAME: _____

LOCATION: _____

VEHICLE MILAGE AT TIME OF SERVICE: [_____ MILES/KM'S]   COST OF SERVICE: [____]

PARTICULARS/DETAILS OF SERVICE:

_____

_____

_____

NEXT SERVICE DUE? [____]

---

DATE SERVICED: _____

SERVICE REPAIR CENTRE NAME: _____

LOCATION: _____

VEHICLE MILAGE AT TIME OF SERVICE: [_____ MILES/KM'S]   COST OF SERVICE: [____]

PARTICULARS/DETAILS OF SERVICE:

_____

_____

_____

NEXT SERVICE DUE? [____]

# MAINTENANCE LOG

DATE SERVICED: _____

SERVICE REPAIR CENTRE NAME: _____

LOCATION: _____

VEHICLE MILAGE AT TIME OF SERVICE: [          ] MILES/KM'S    COST OF SERVICE: [     ]

PARTICULARS/DETAILS OF SERVICE:

_____
_____
_____

NEXT SERVICE DUE? [          ]

- - - - - - - - - - - - - - - - - - - - - - - - - - - - - - - - - - - - - - - -

DATE SERVICED: _____

SERVICE REPAIR CENTRE NAME: _____

LOCATION: _____

VEHICLE MILAGE AT TIME OF SERVICE: [          ] MILES/KM'S    COST OF SERVICE: [     ]

PARTICULARS/DETAILS OF SERVICE:

_____
_____
_____

NEXT SERVICE DUE? [          ]

Thank you so much for purchasing The Camping Journal.

If you had the opportunity to provide a review online that would be greatly appreciated.

Thank you!

# The Life Graduate Publishing Group

**To see more books that may be of interest to you, please visit www.thelifegraduate/bookstore**

www.ingramcontent.com/pod-product-compliance
Lightning Source LLC
LaVergne TN
LVHW060158080526
838202LV00052B/4169